Colorful Portraits of Autumn

book & photography by
Jodi Marie Fisher

all photographs taken in the Northwestern United States

Copyright © 2019 Jodi Marie Fisher
Photography by Jodi Marie Fisher

All rights reserved. This book or any portion thereof may not be reproduced or used in any manner whatsoever without the express written permission of the publisher.

Printed in the United States of America
First Edition 2019
Colorful Portraits of Autumn

ISBN-13: 978-1710969184
ISBN-10: 1710969180

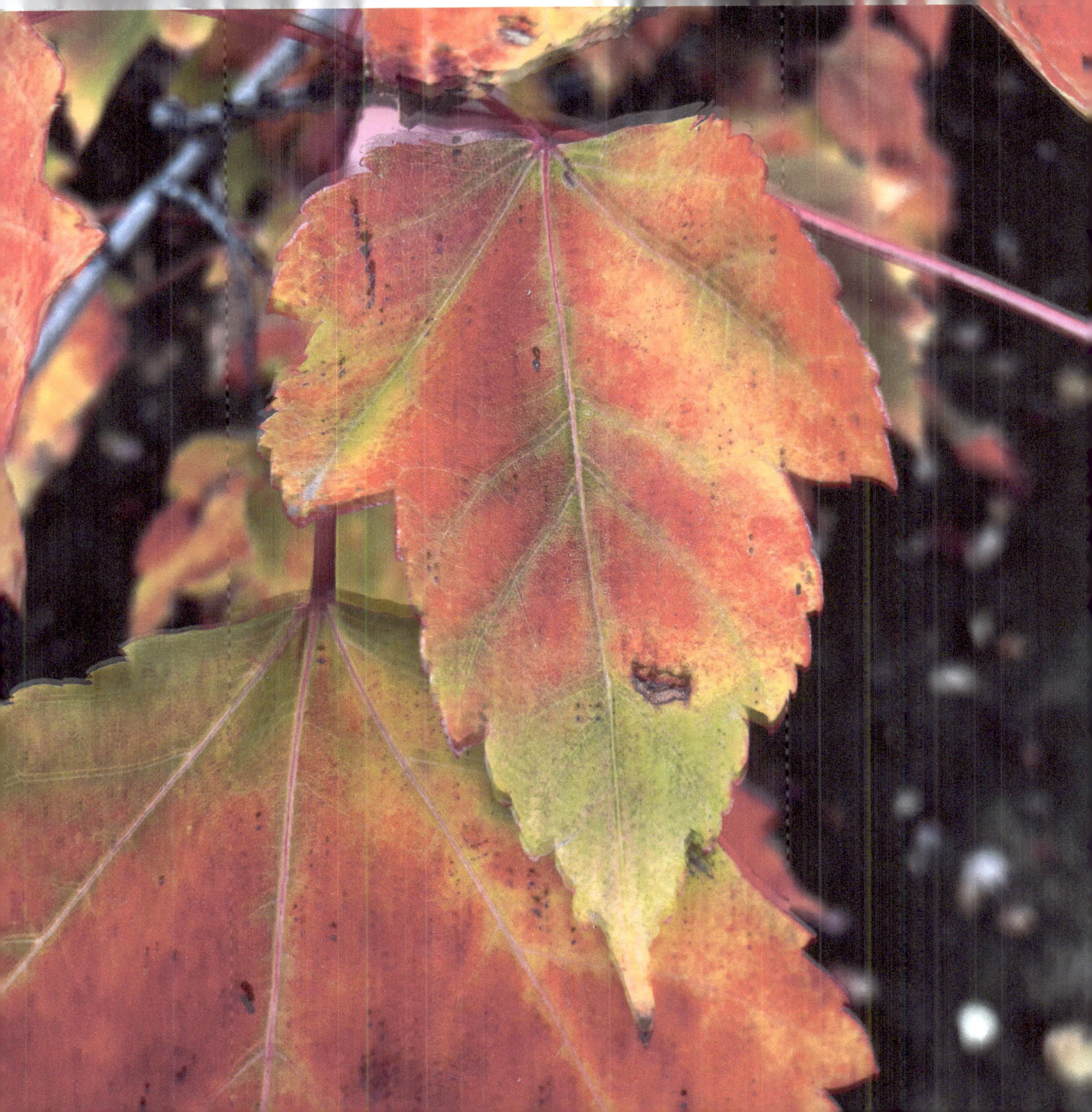

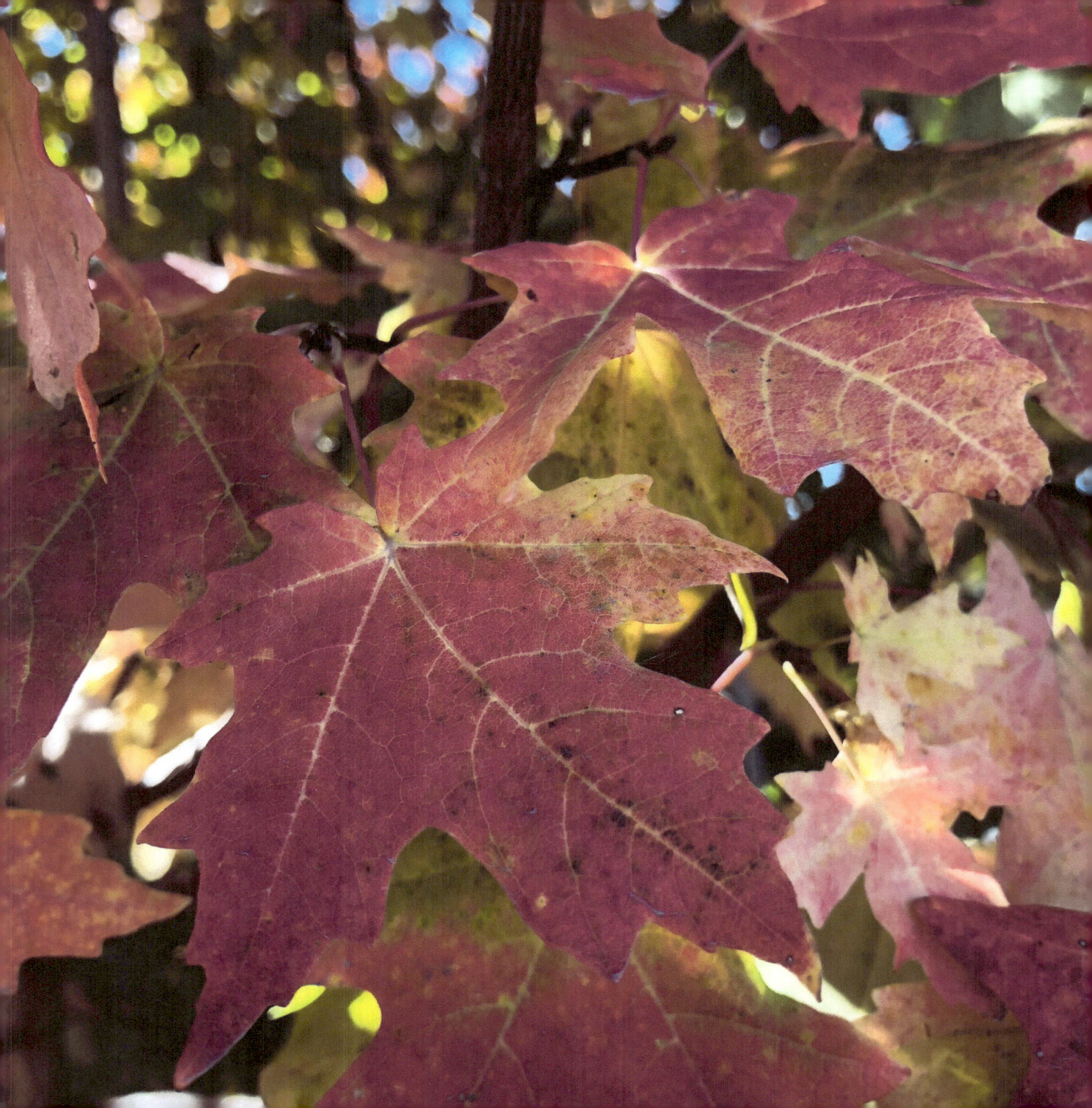

What are Colorful portraits of autumn?

Seasons have portraits. **Faces. Personalities. Characteristics** you can recognize. When you see a familiar face. A family member. A friend. Even a stranger. Their portrait is distinct. Though some are similar and many almost the same, no one face is the same in people and the same is true in portraits of nature.

This book of colorful portraits of nature displays many, yet certainly not even close to all, of some of the faces you recognize in autumn. In autumn, more than in any other season, we start to look more closely at the leaves around us. The leaves on the trees. The leaves barely hanging on. The leaves that fall and paint the ground in rainbow colors. Among those leaves too, we see little differences that make each one special and unique.

And yet, as I look out, I start to see a little more how all the faces of each unique leaf join together to create a beautiful canvas. When you look at one leaf by itself, you see one face. Together, you see fire, light, and deep colors amongst the decaying, drying, cold announcement of the season to come.

With other seasons also come change, but in autumn we anticipate the change more. We expect it. We more readily welcome the change in its marvelous beauty.

In life, there is autumn too. Our faces whither, decay, grow old, and change over time. Our face ten years ago may not tell the story that our face tells today. Yet, each stage of our life and each version of ourselves is beautiful and must be celebrated.

Keep watch through these pages for autumn characteristics in not just the iconic colorful autumn leaves, but also in trees, pine needles, seed pods, pine cones, acorns, fruits, vines, flower buds, and autumn flowers such as dahlias, chrysanthemums, and the remaining and decaying roses and rose buds.

Open your eyes and welcome the change. As you do, allow yourself time to reflect. Time to grow. Time to let go.

Thank you for picking up this book and experiencing these portraits together.

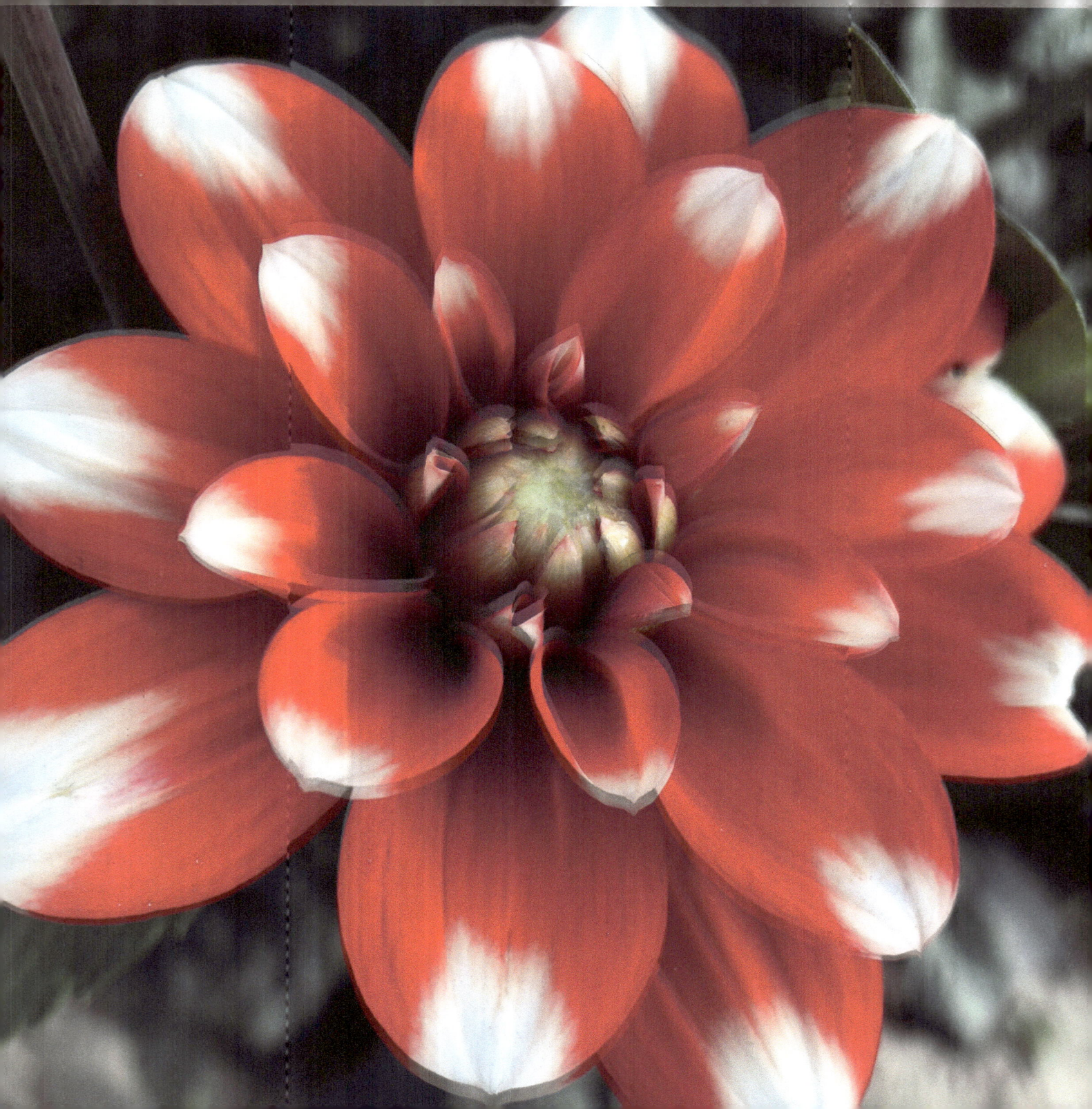

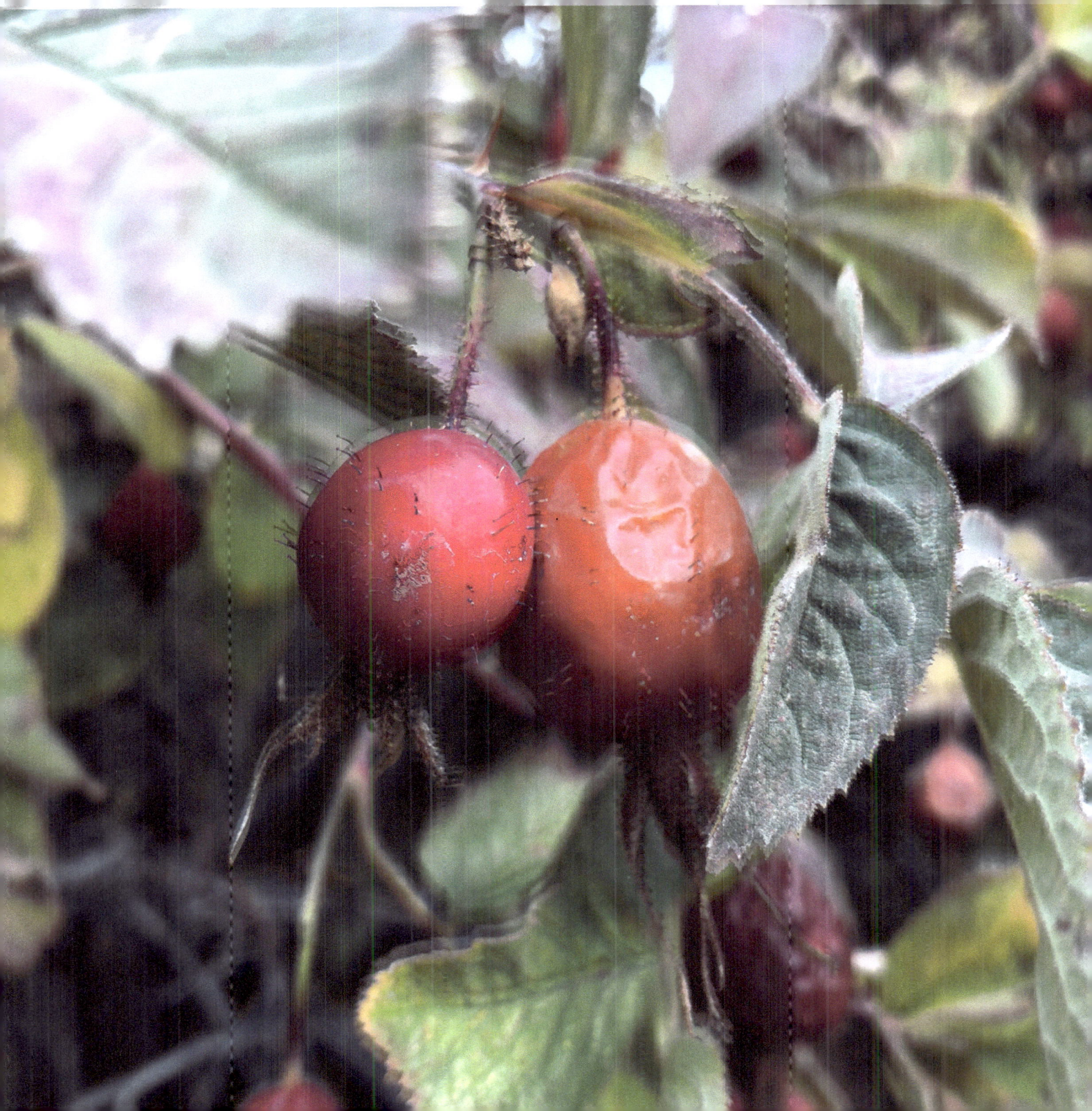

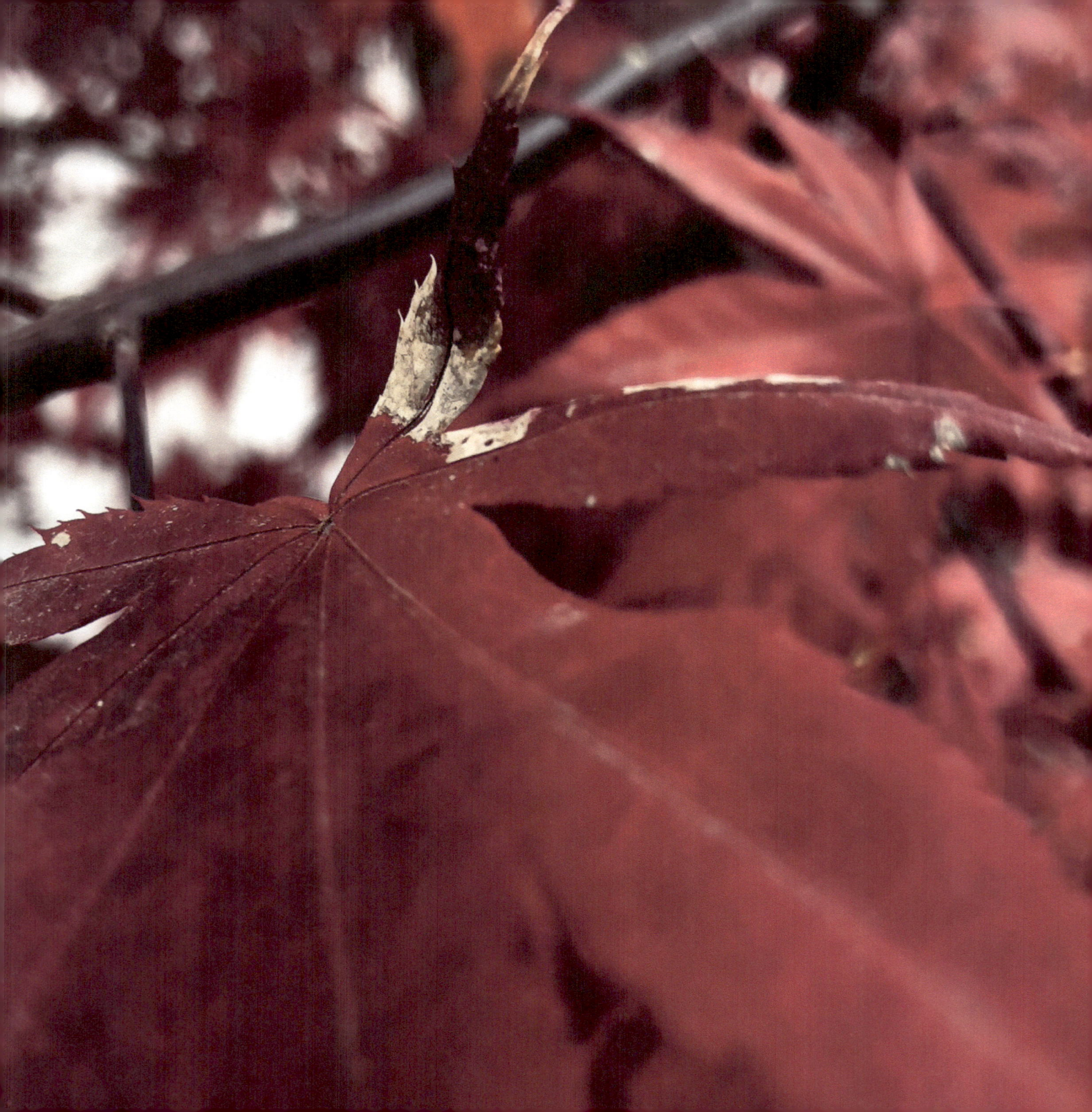

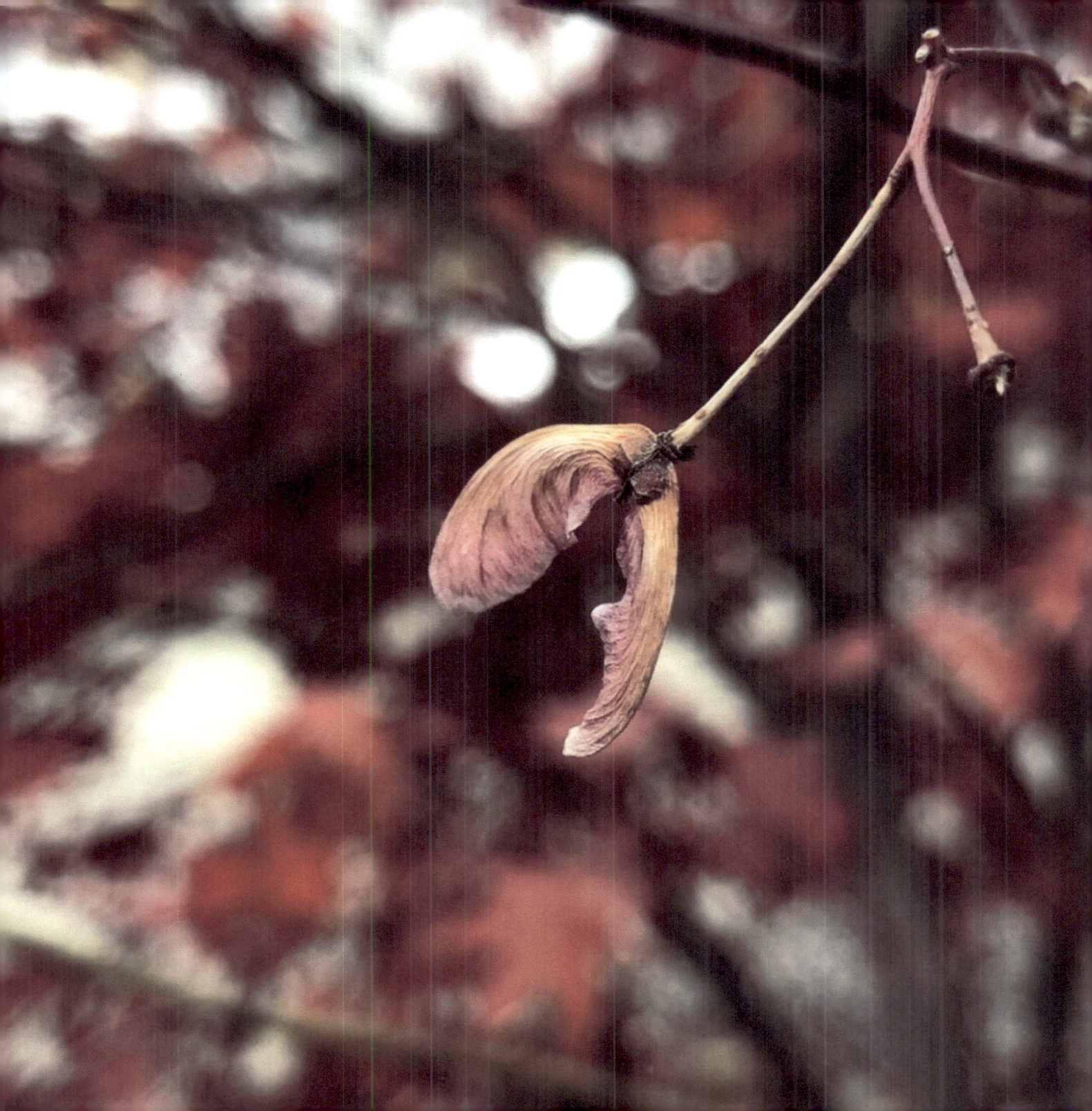

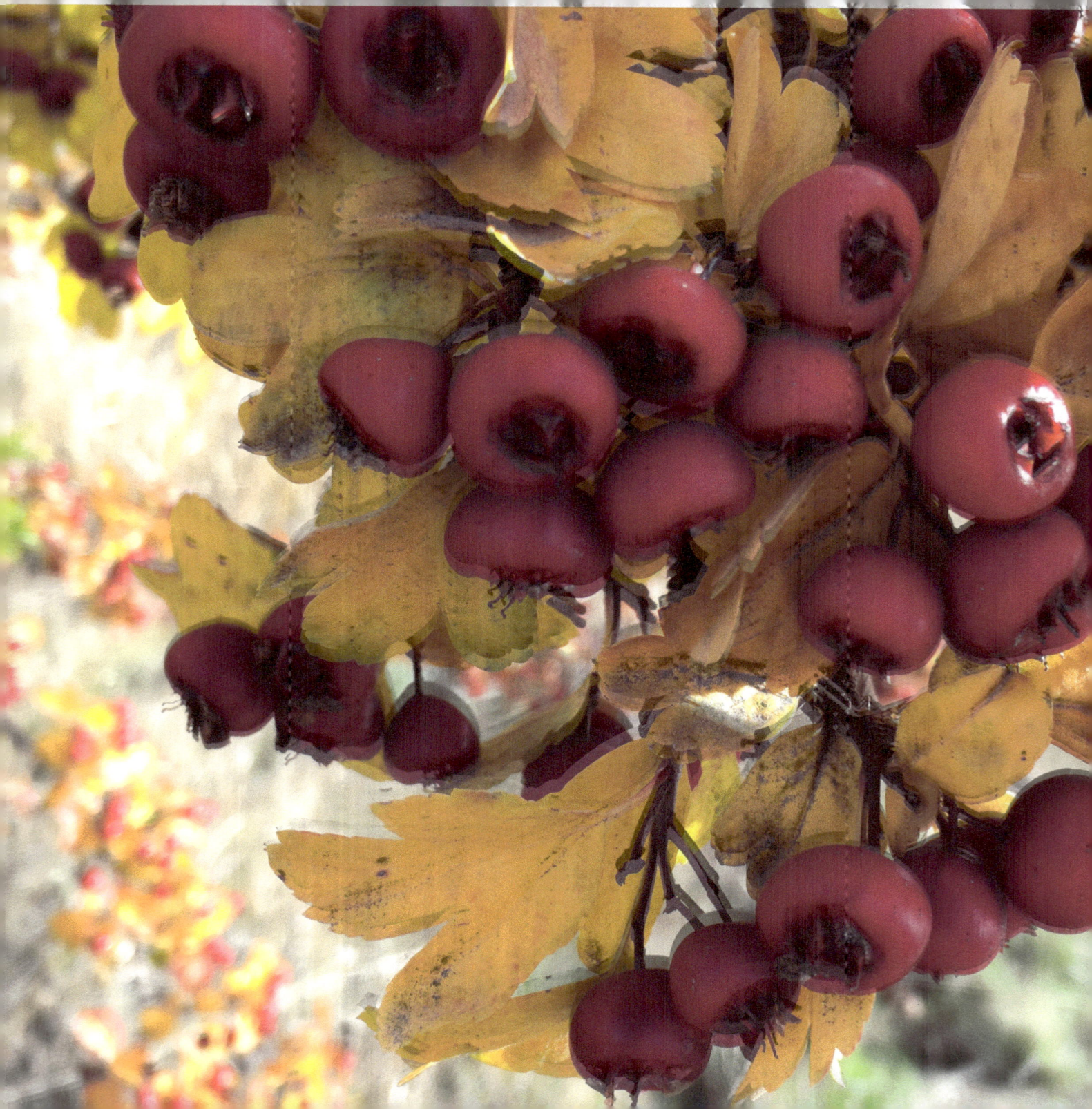

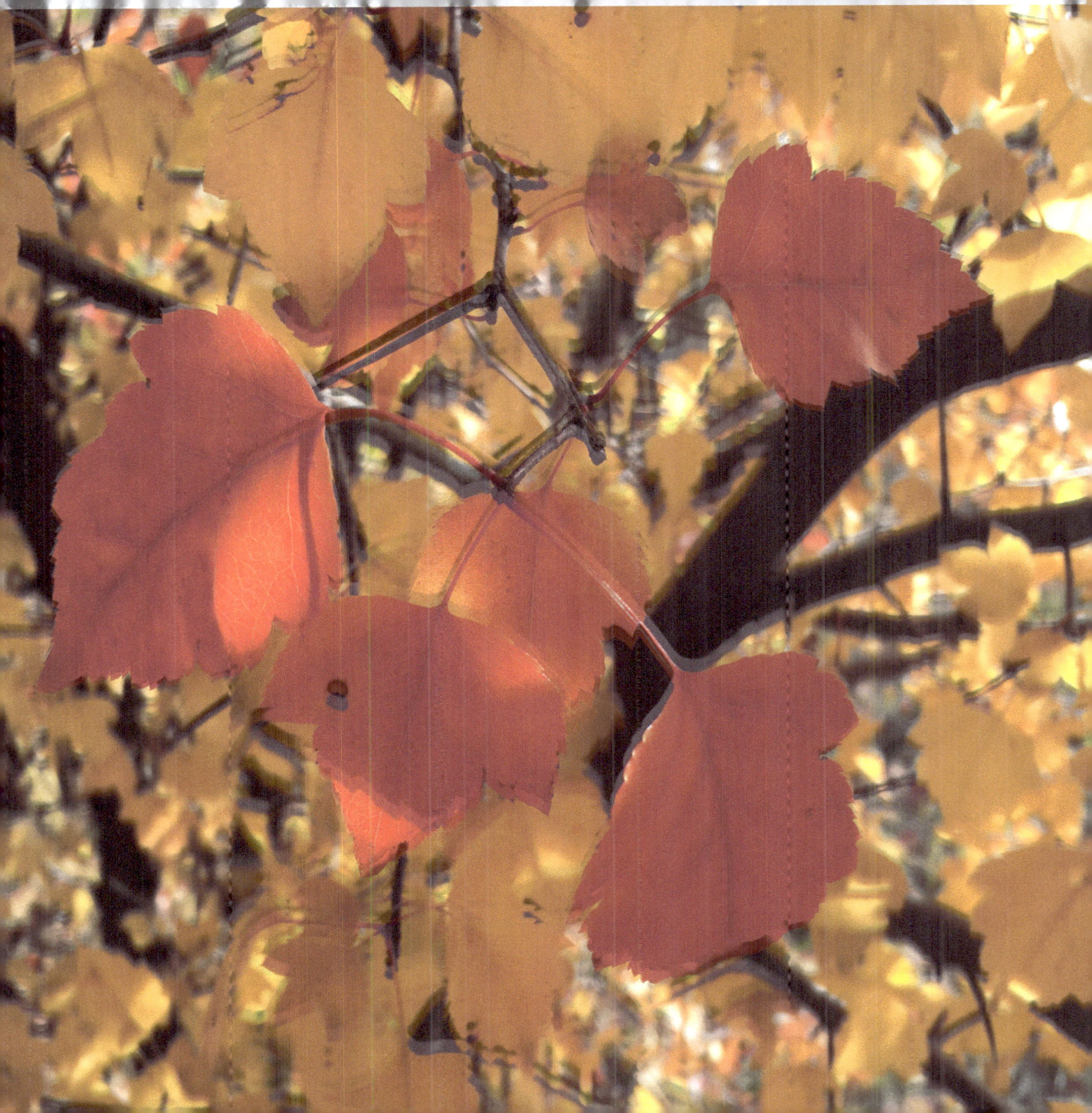

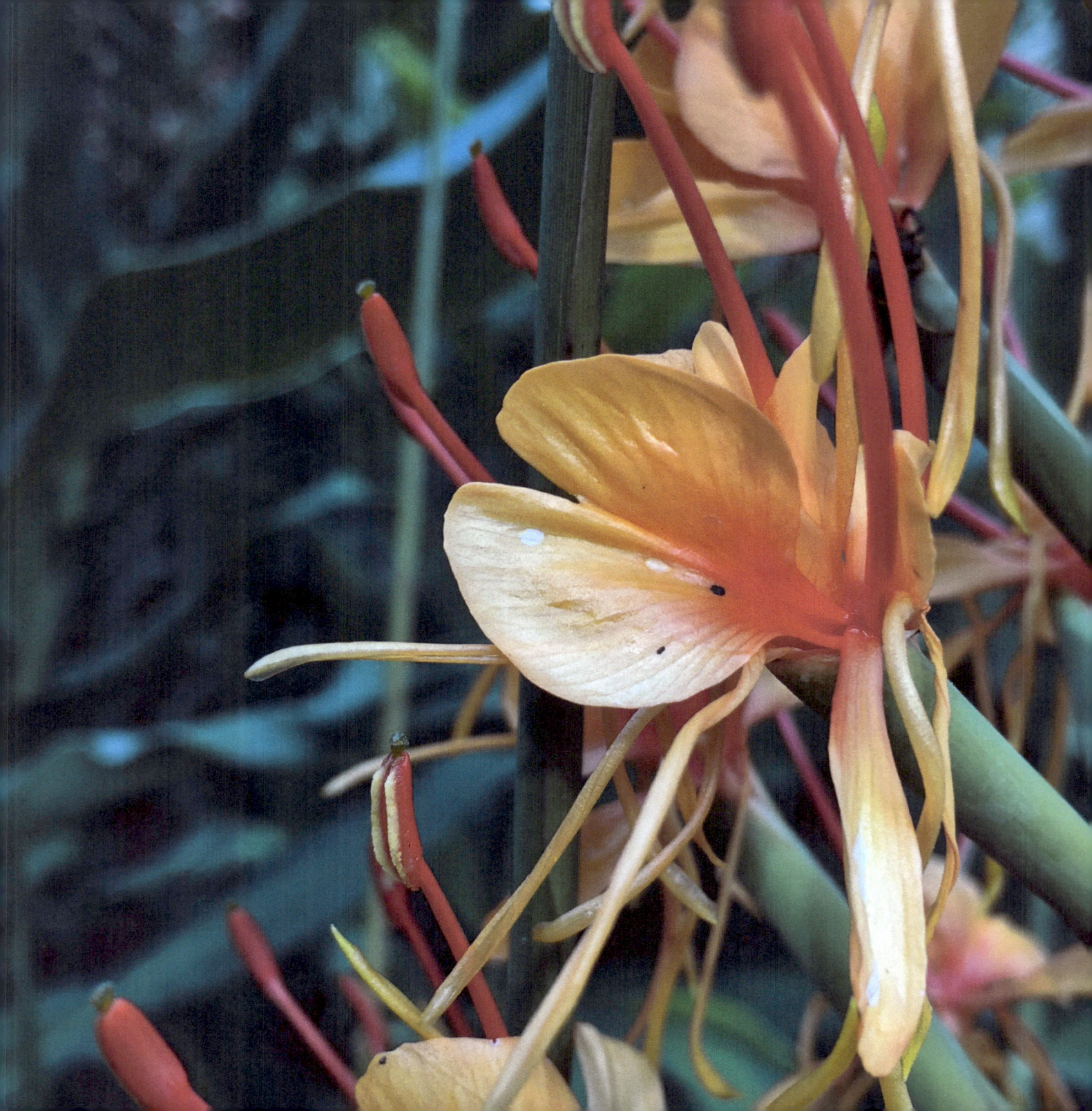

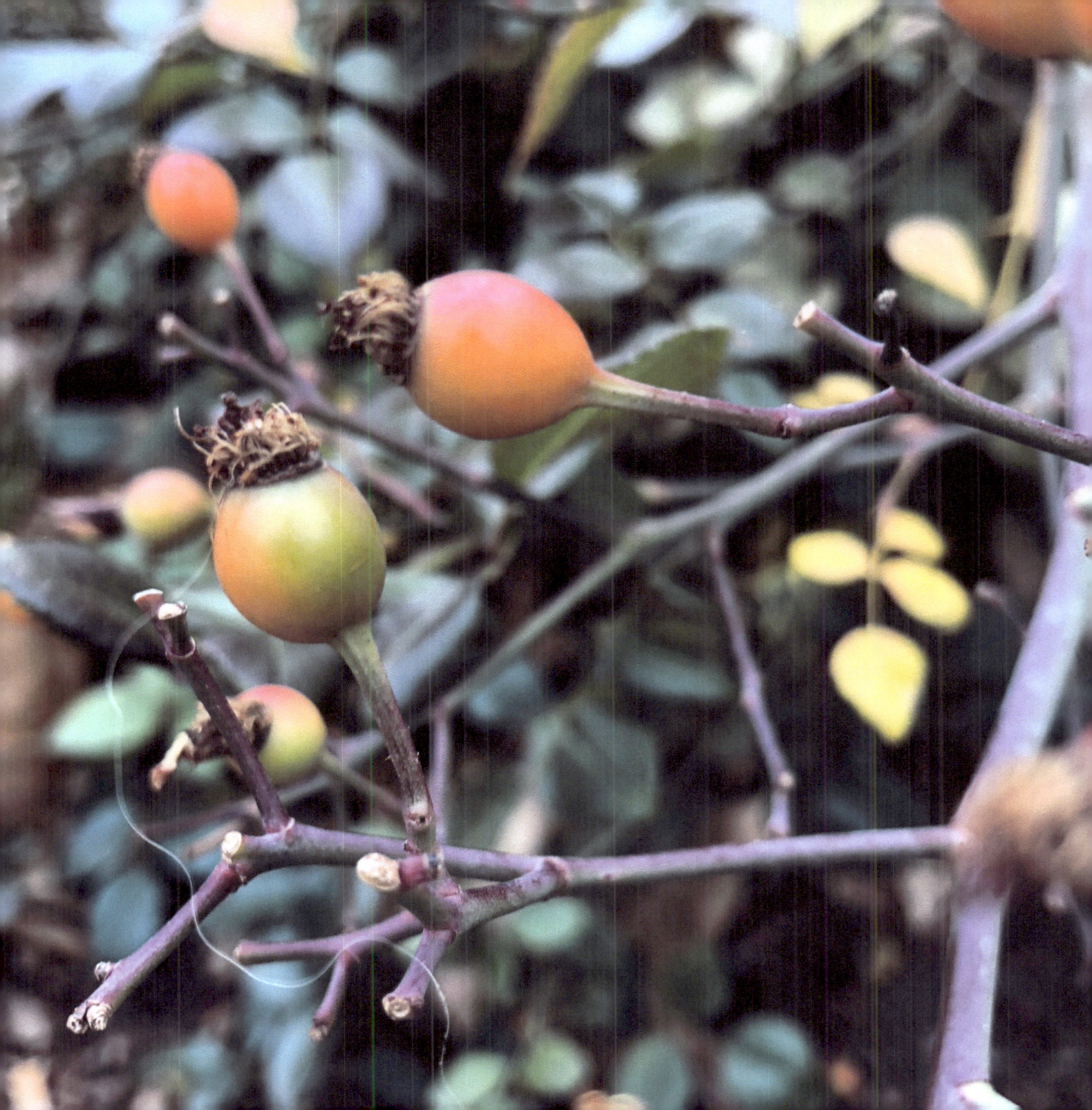

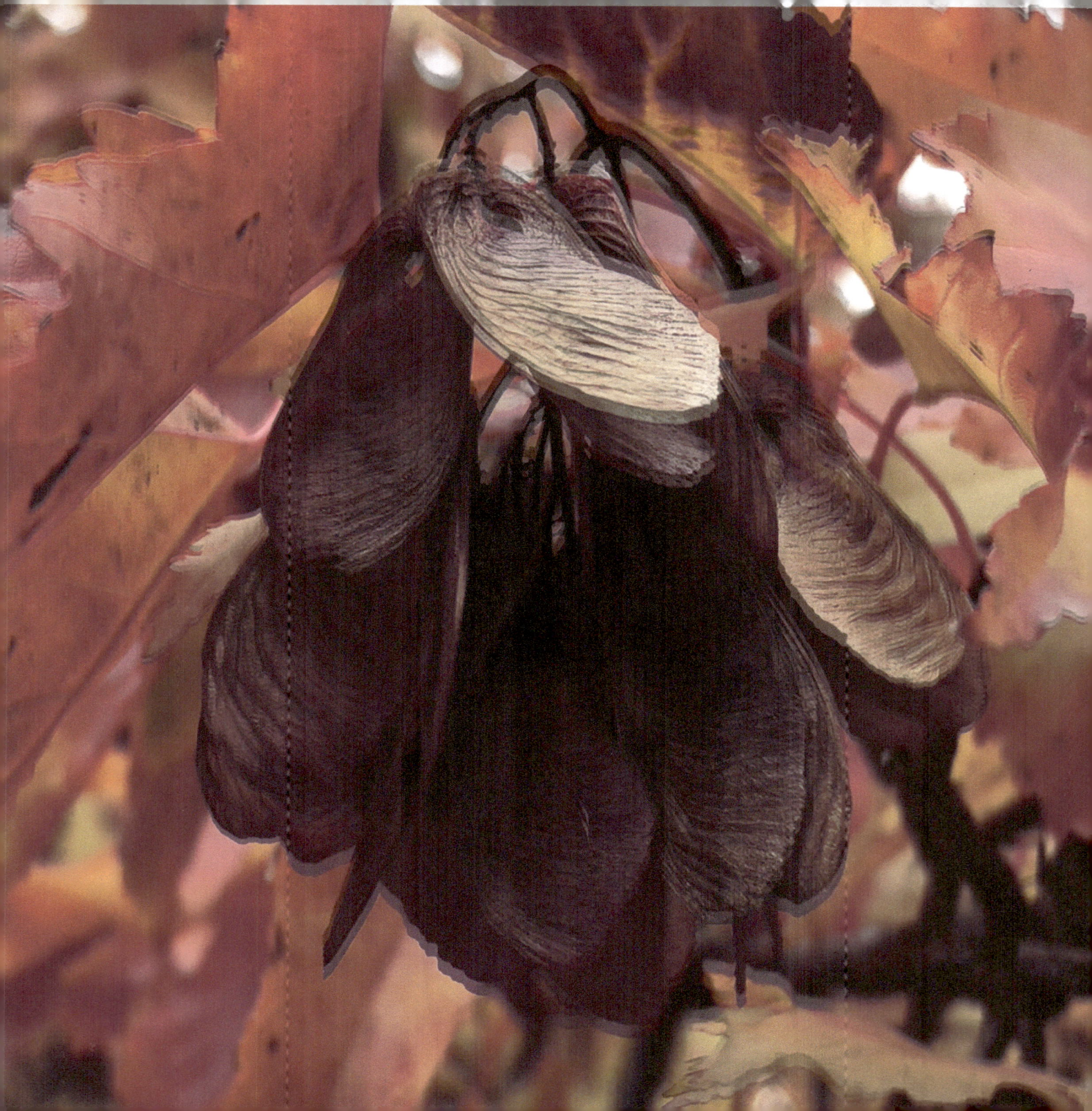

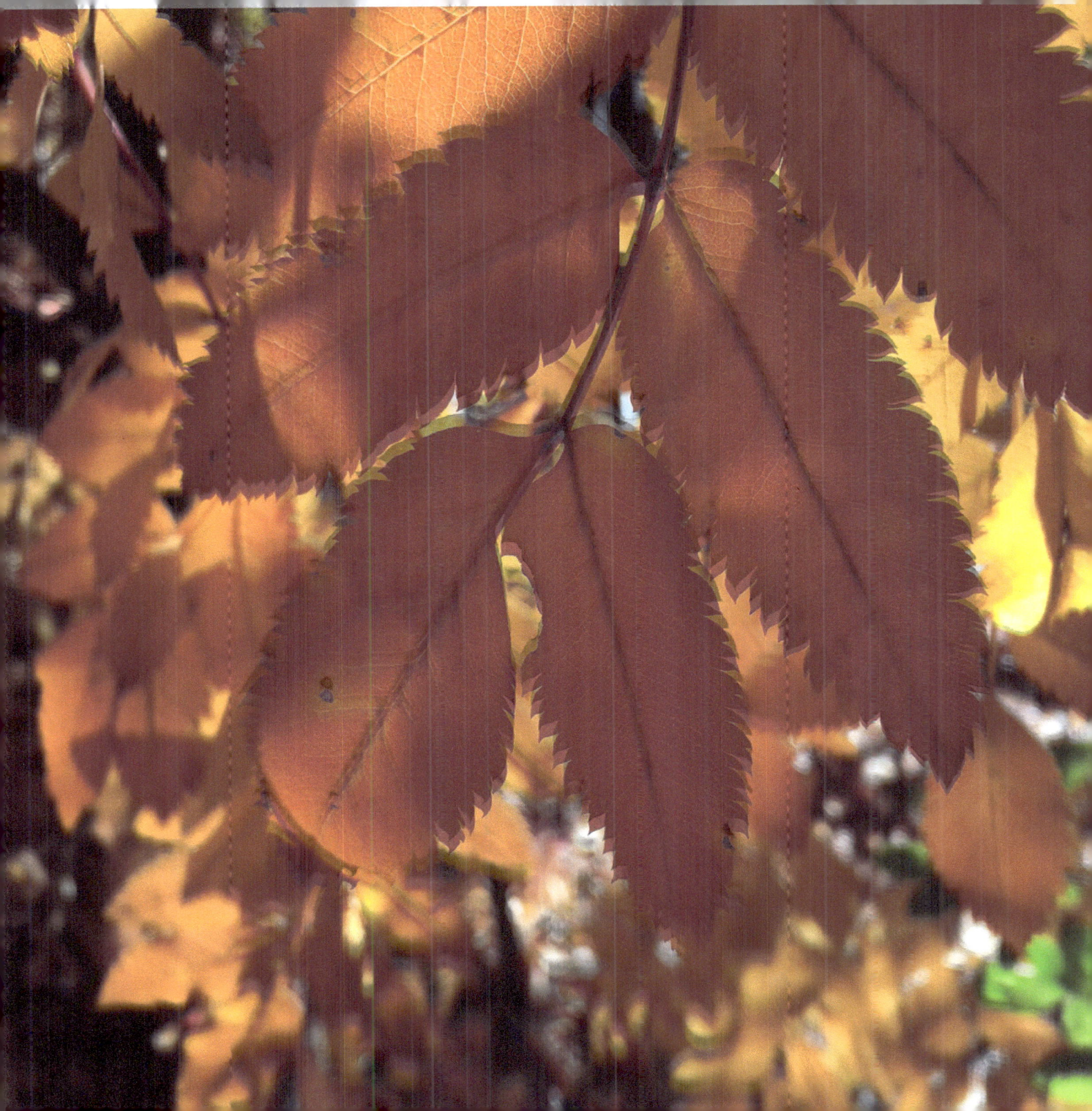

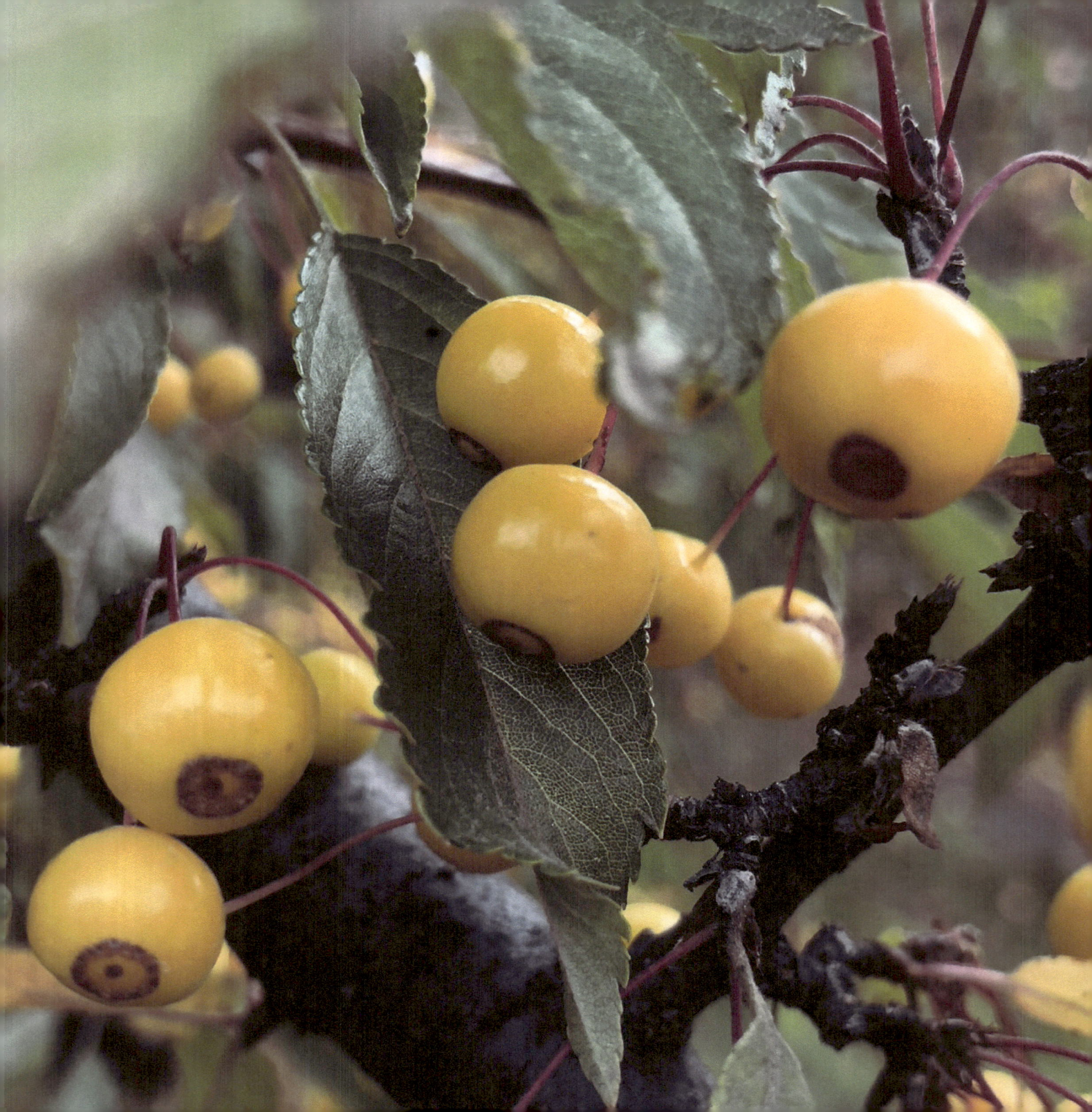

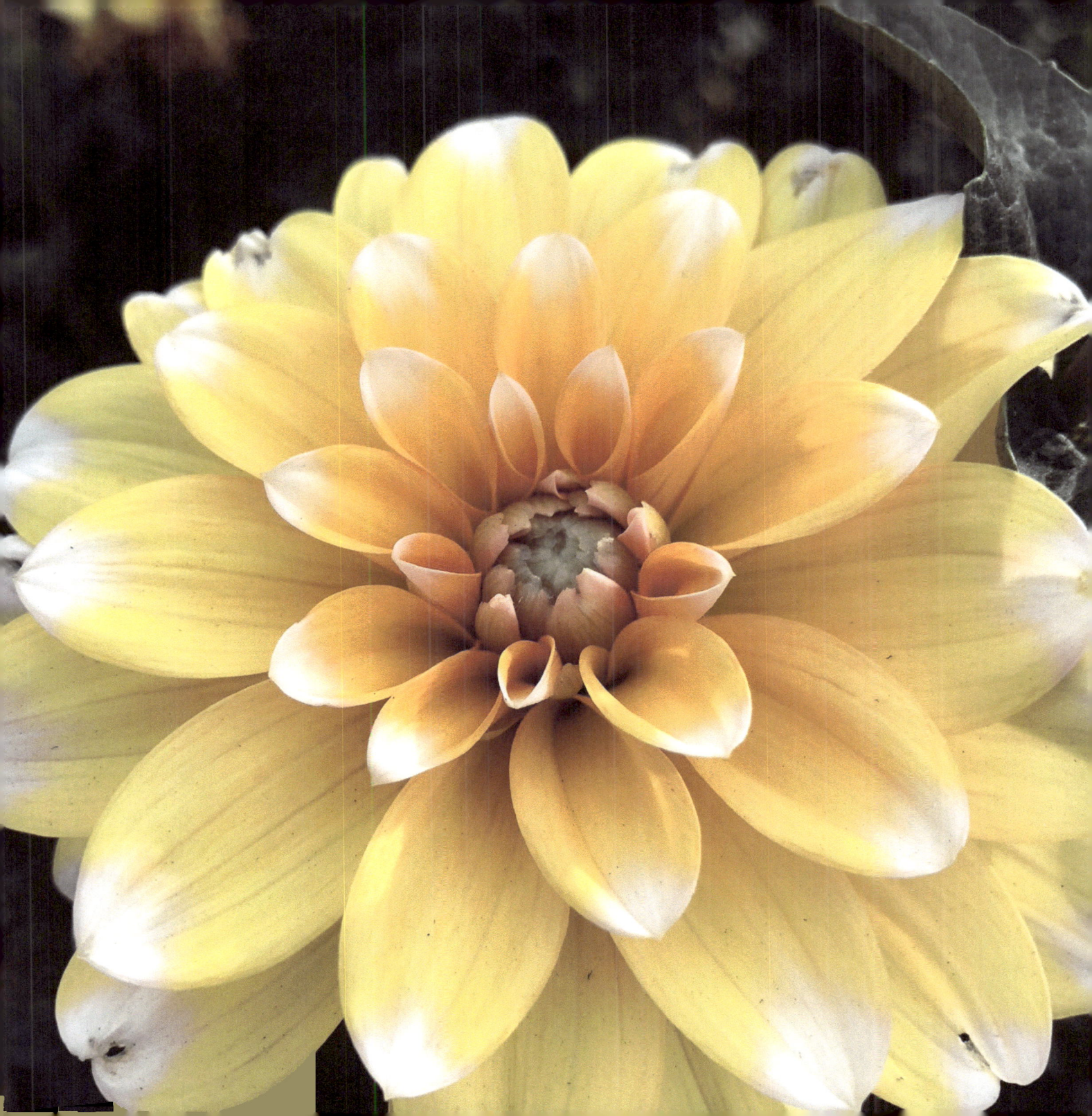

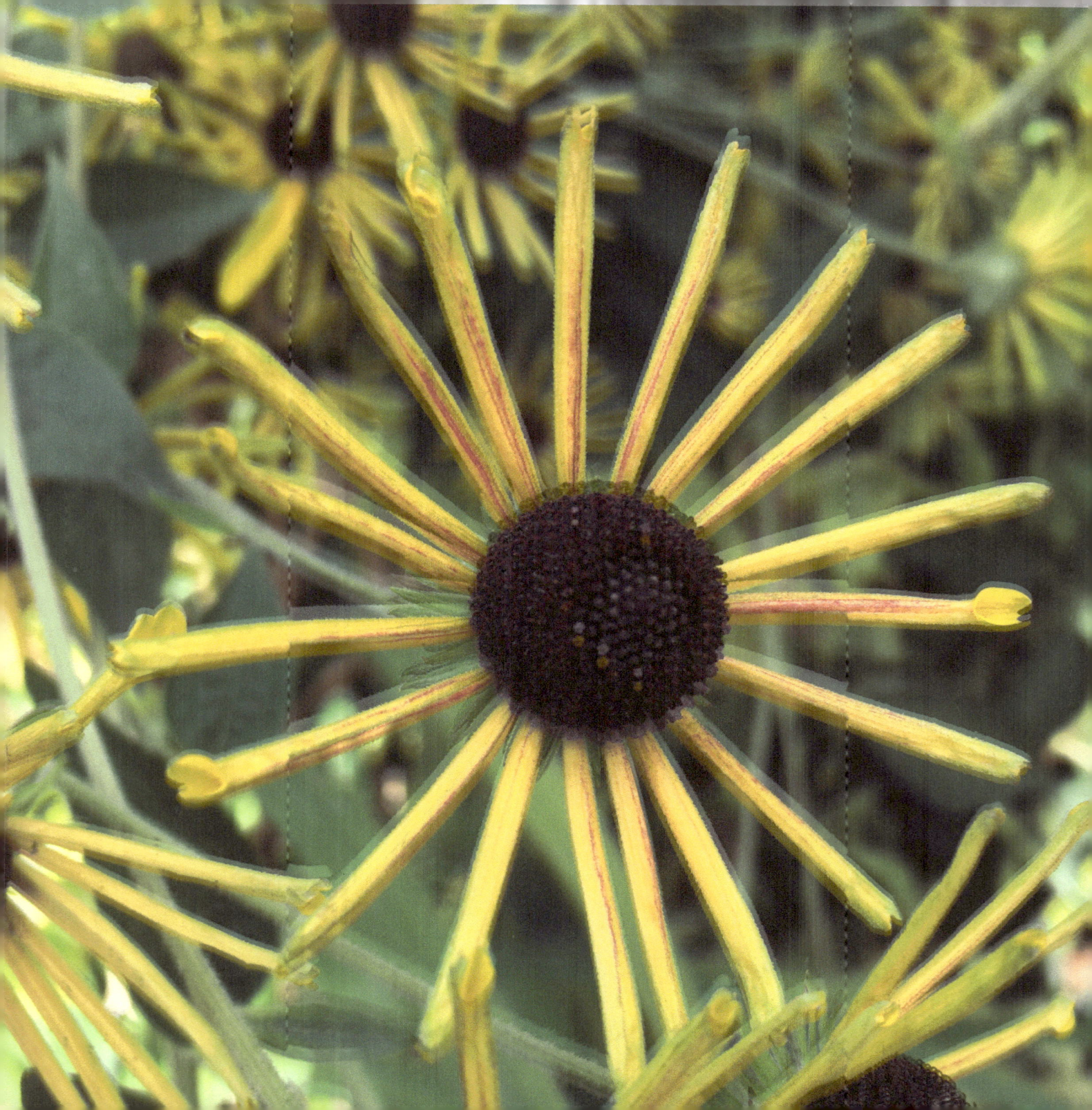

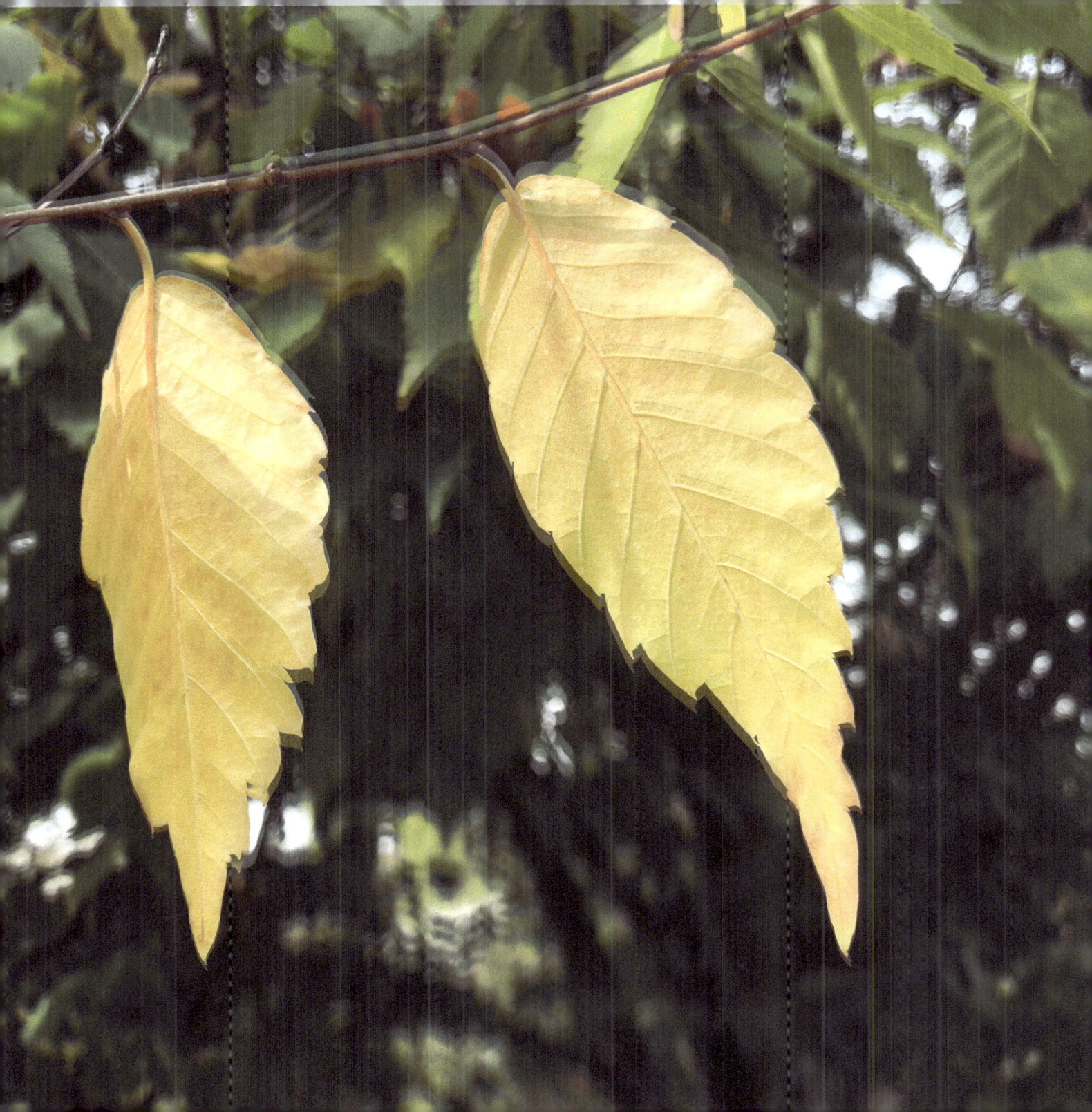

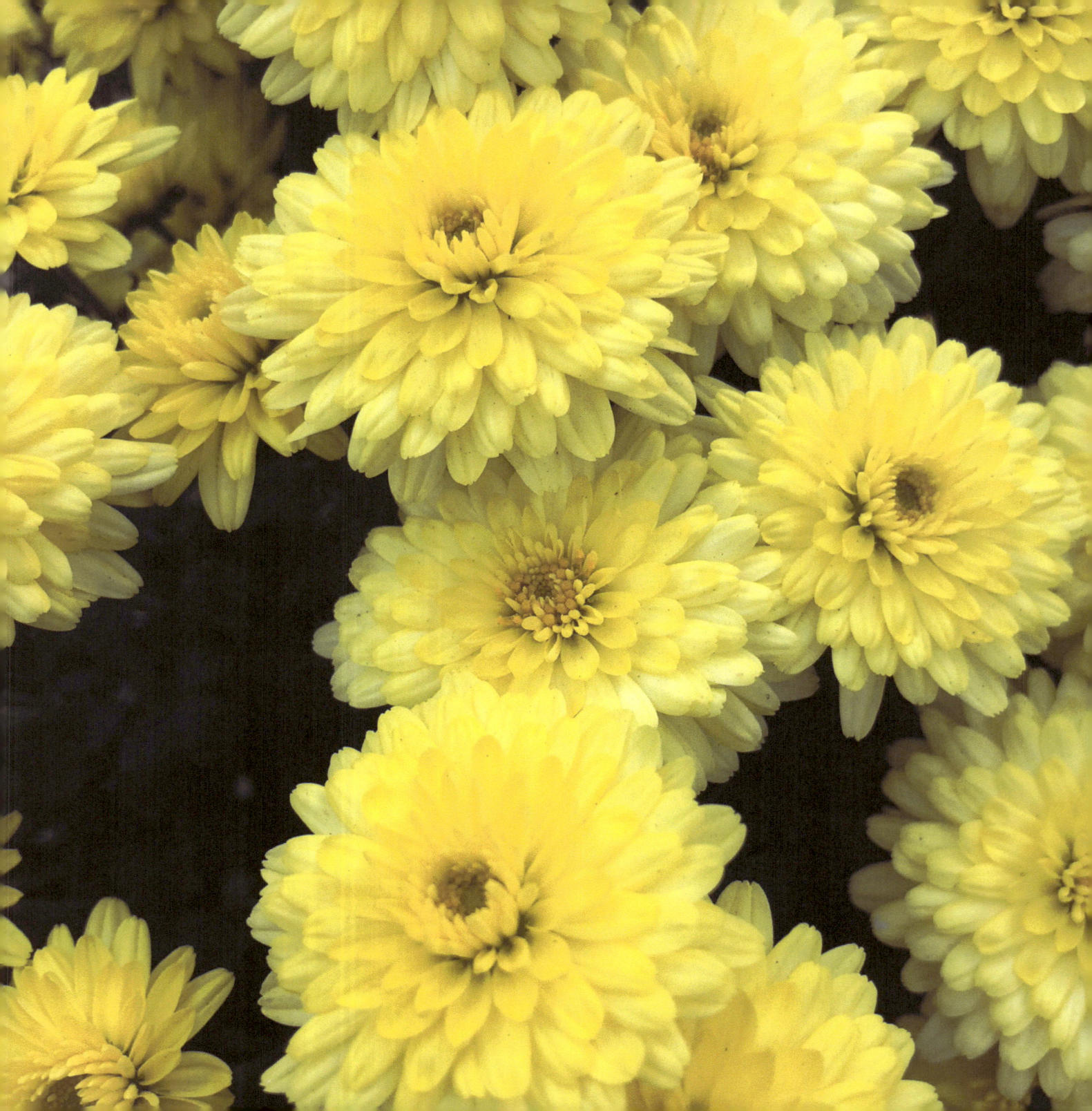

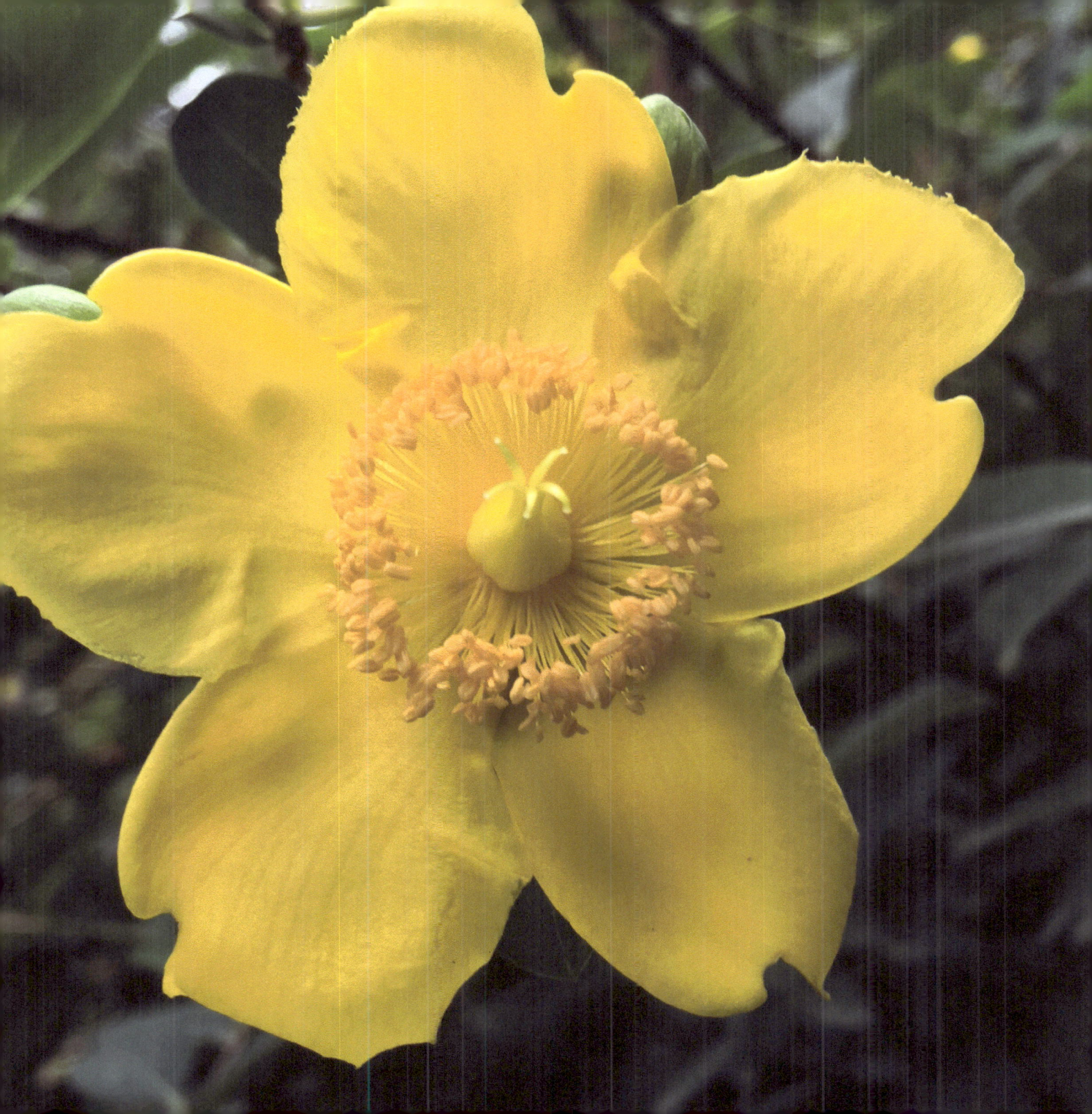

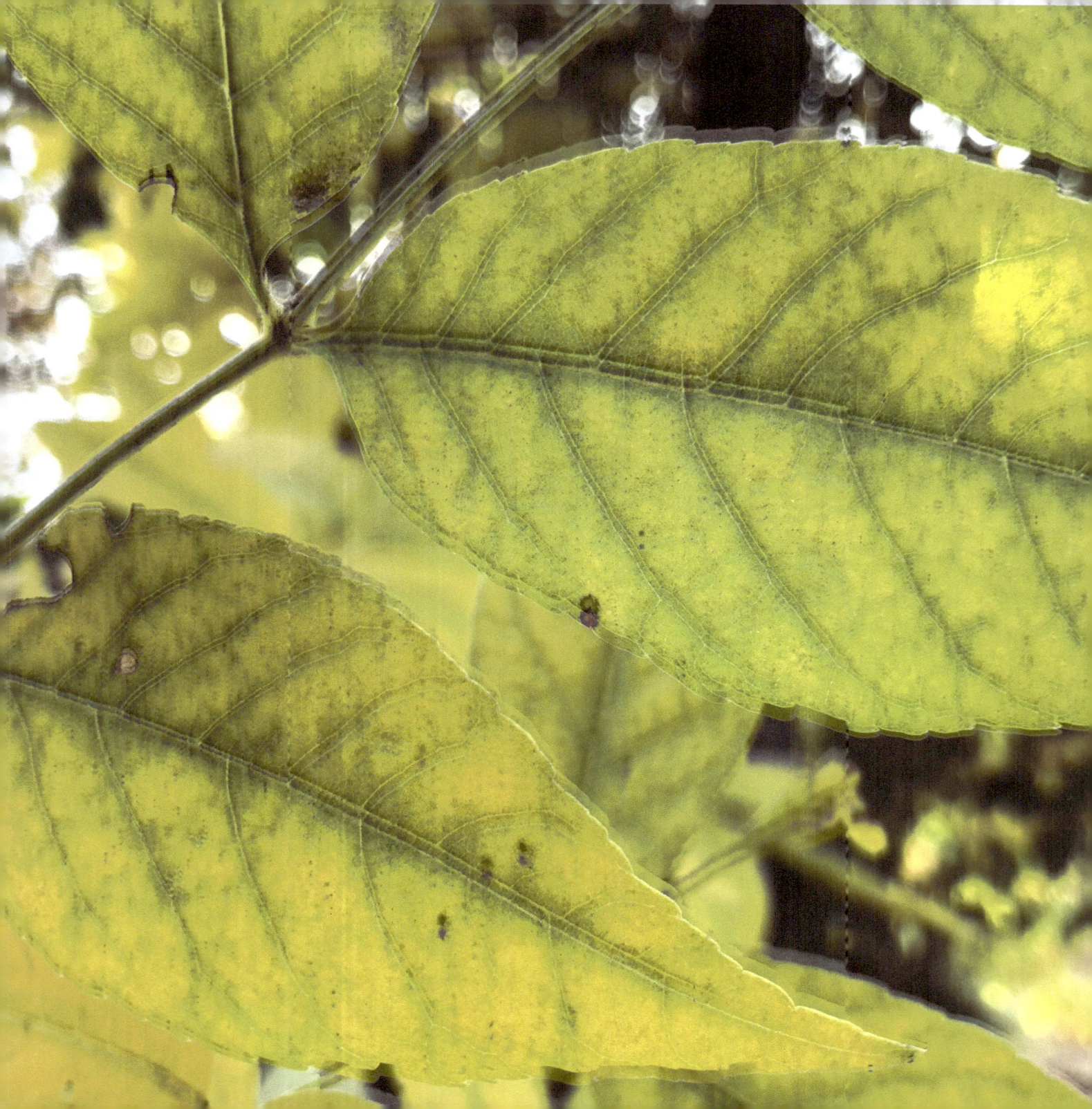

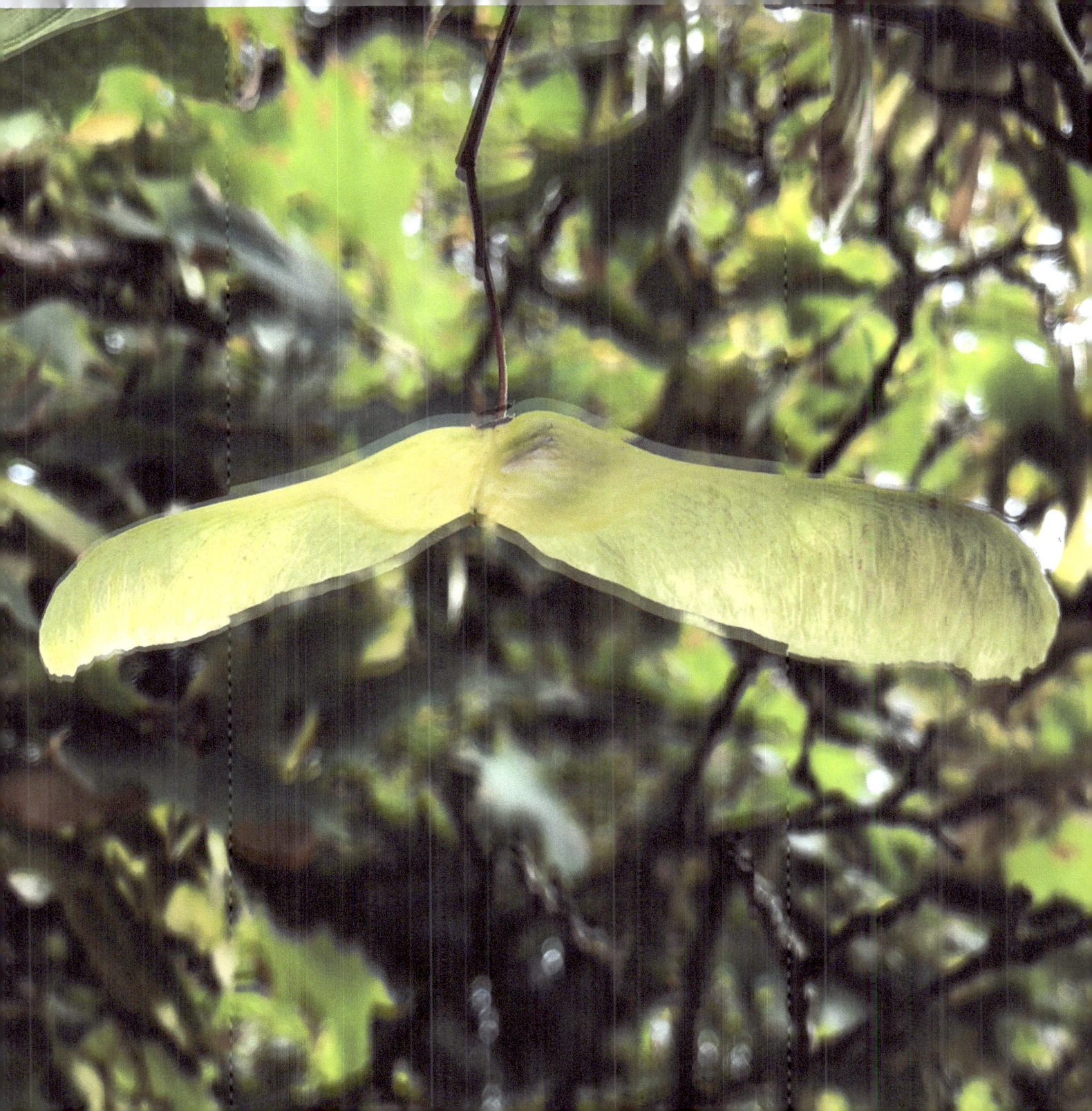

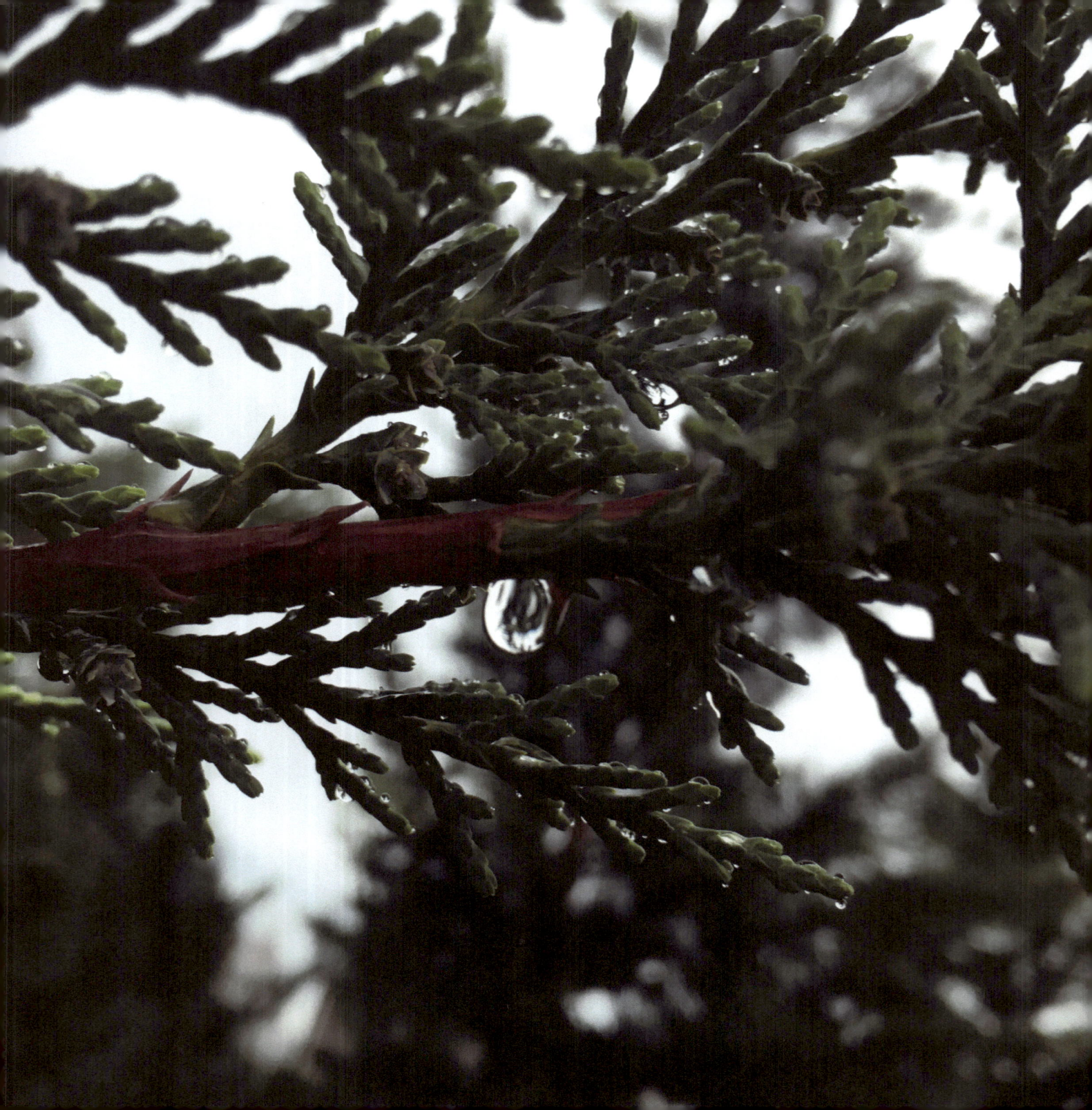

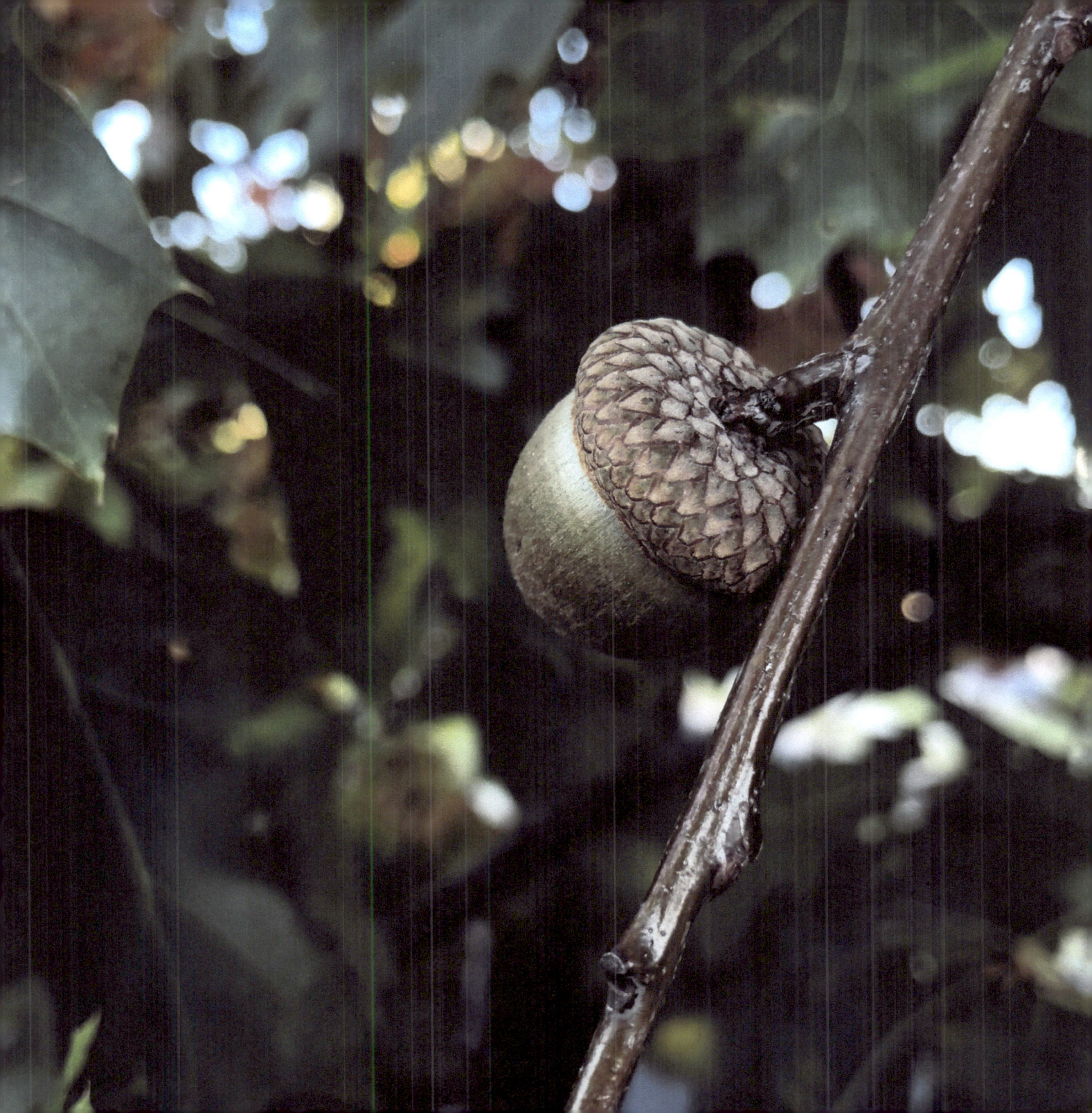

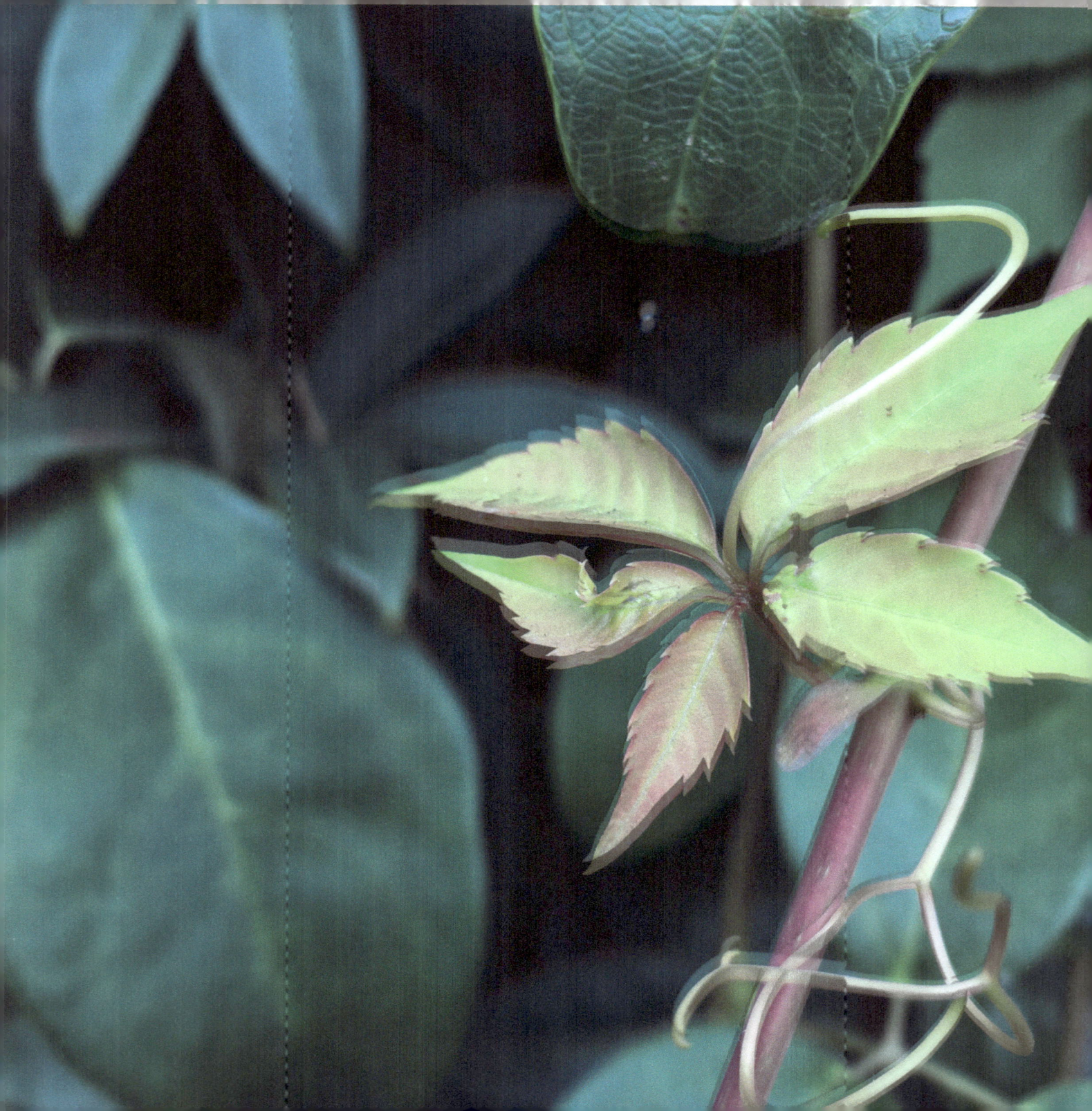

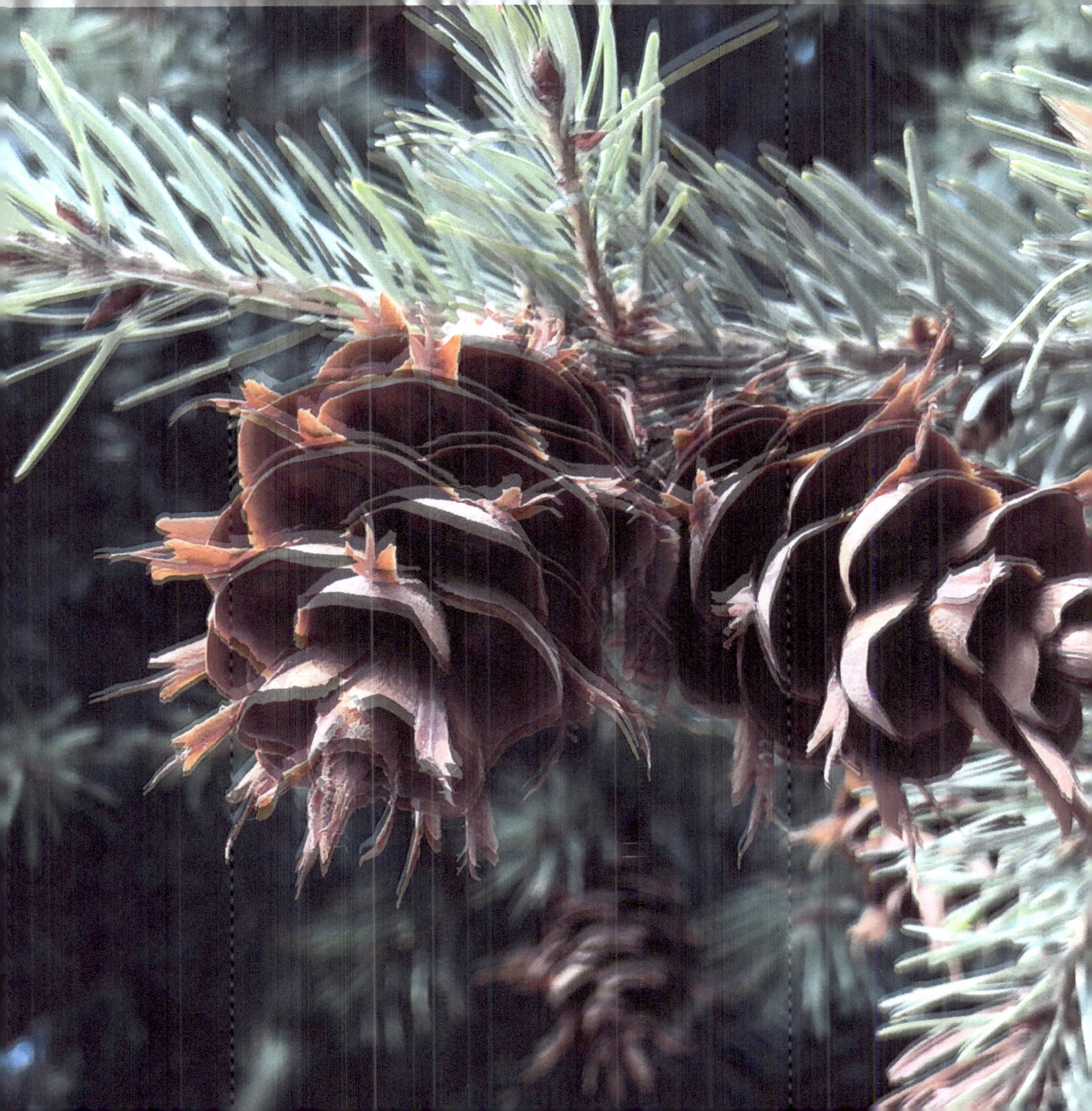

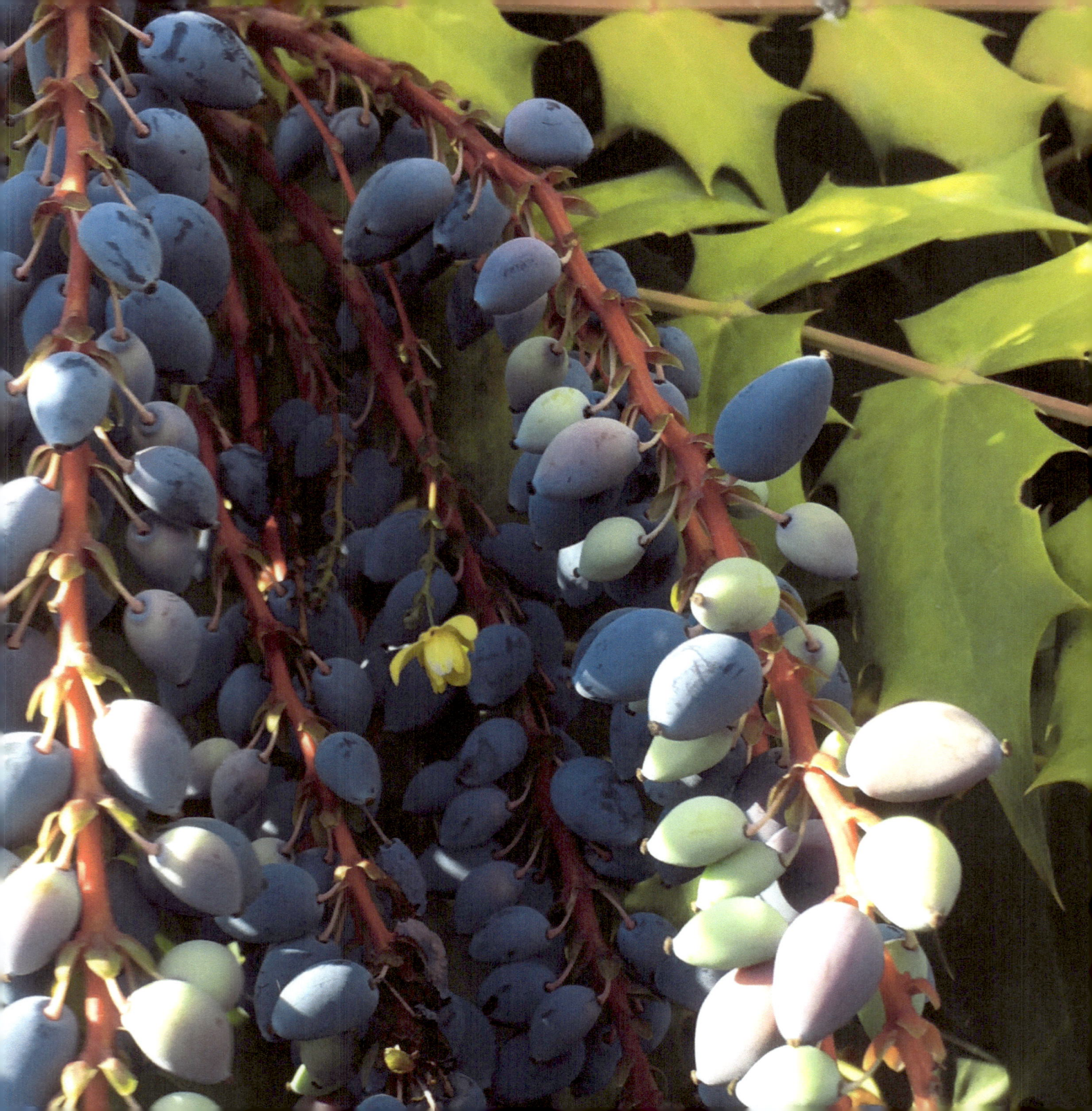

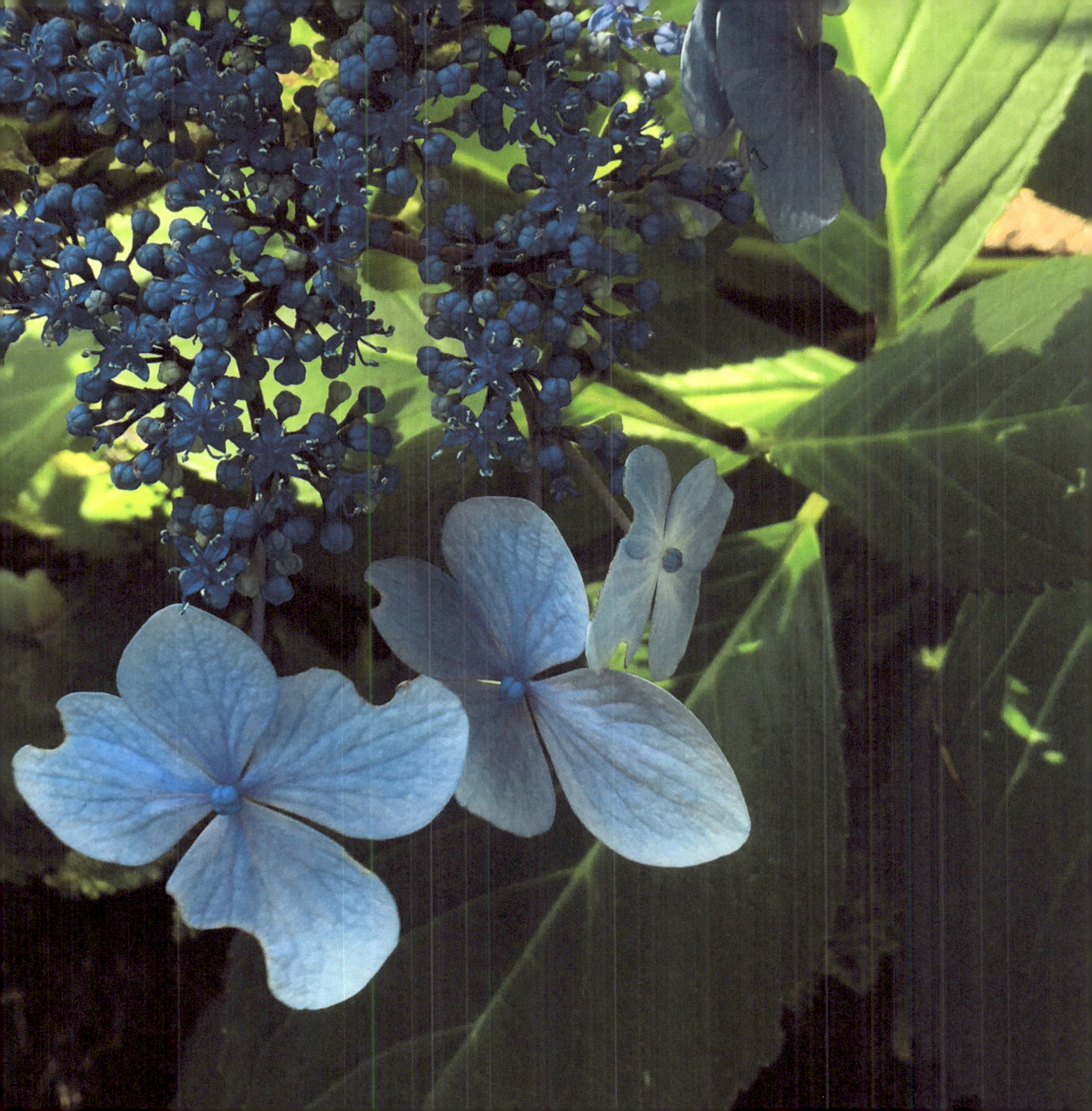

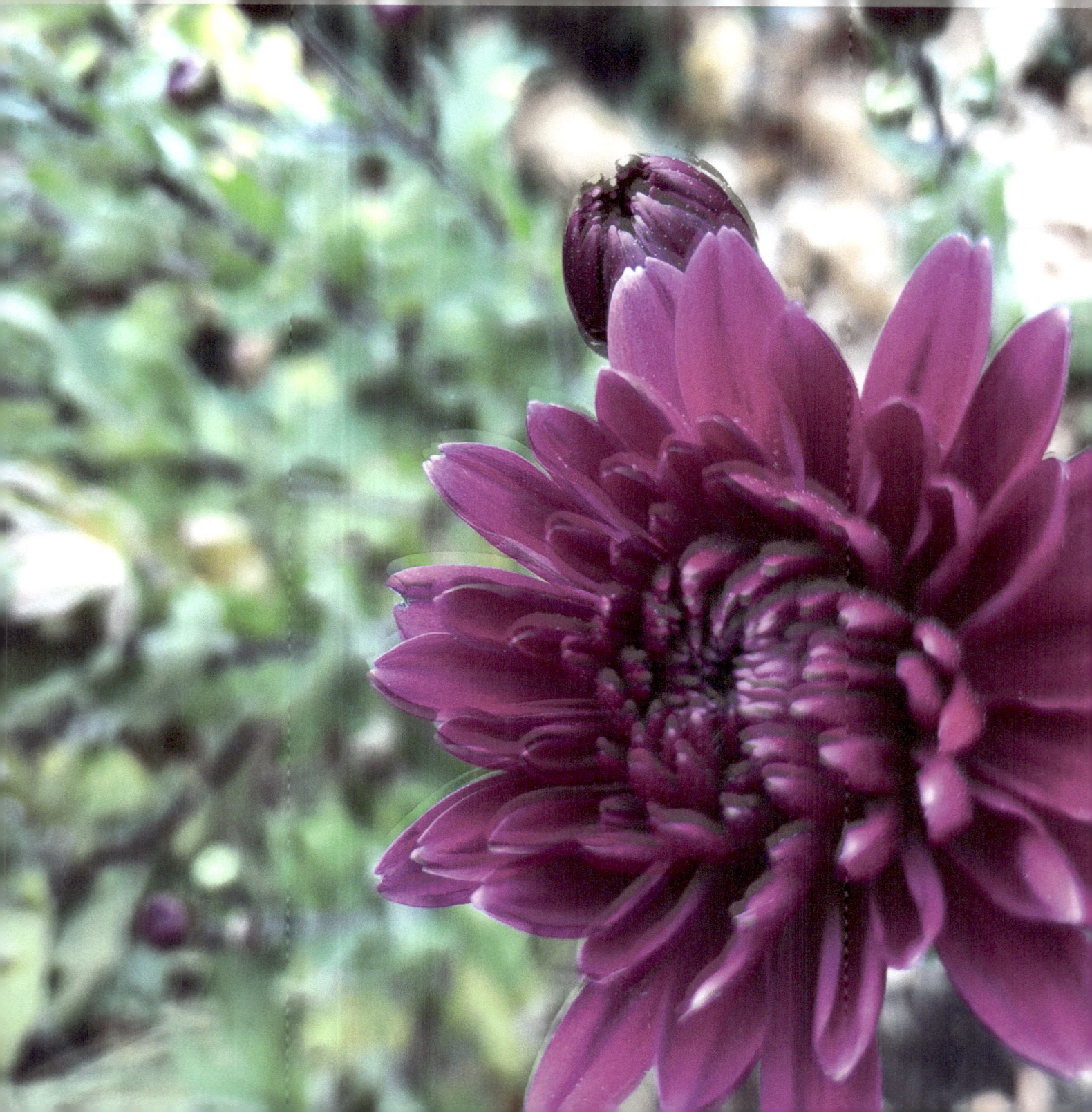

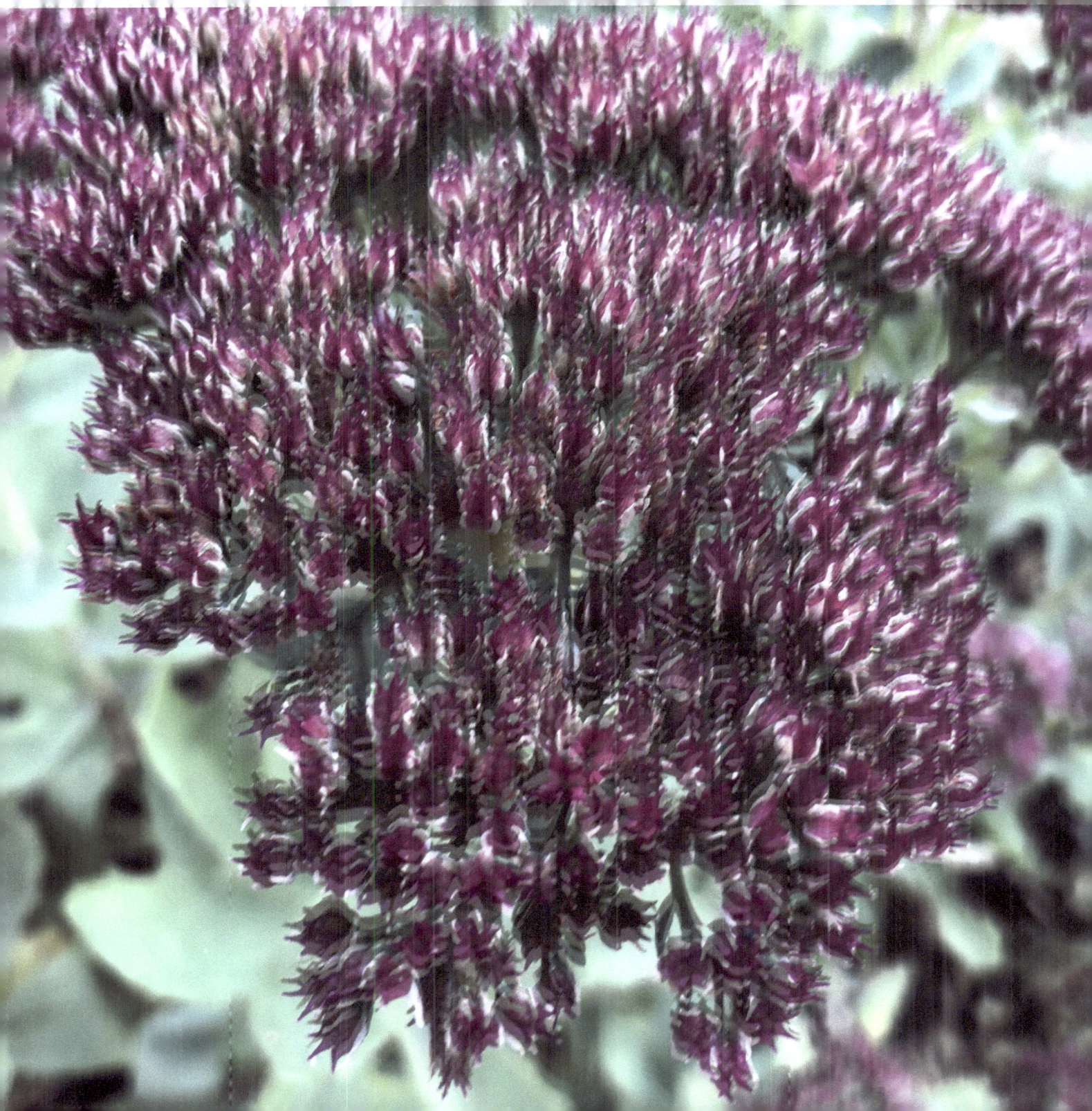

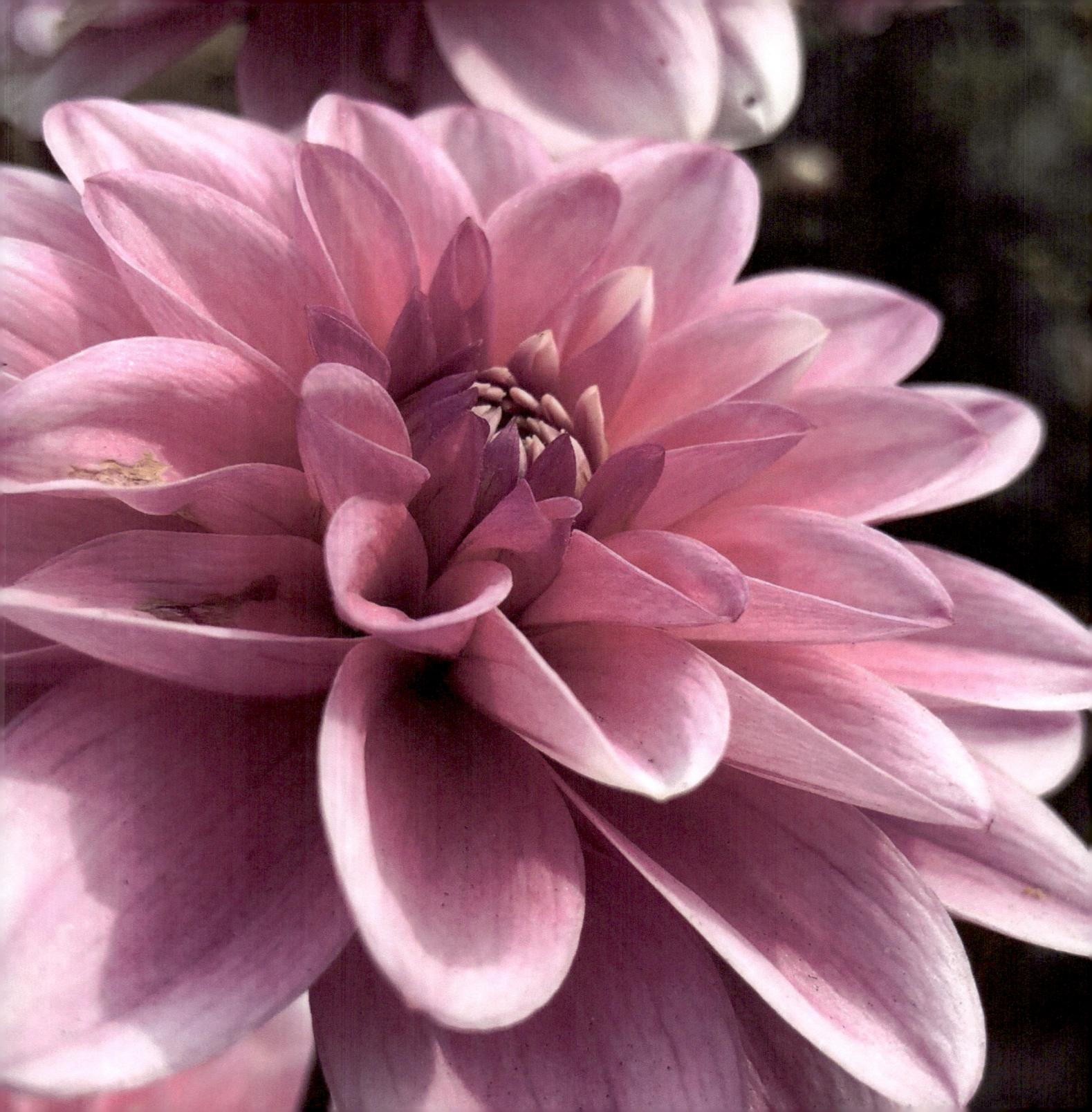

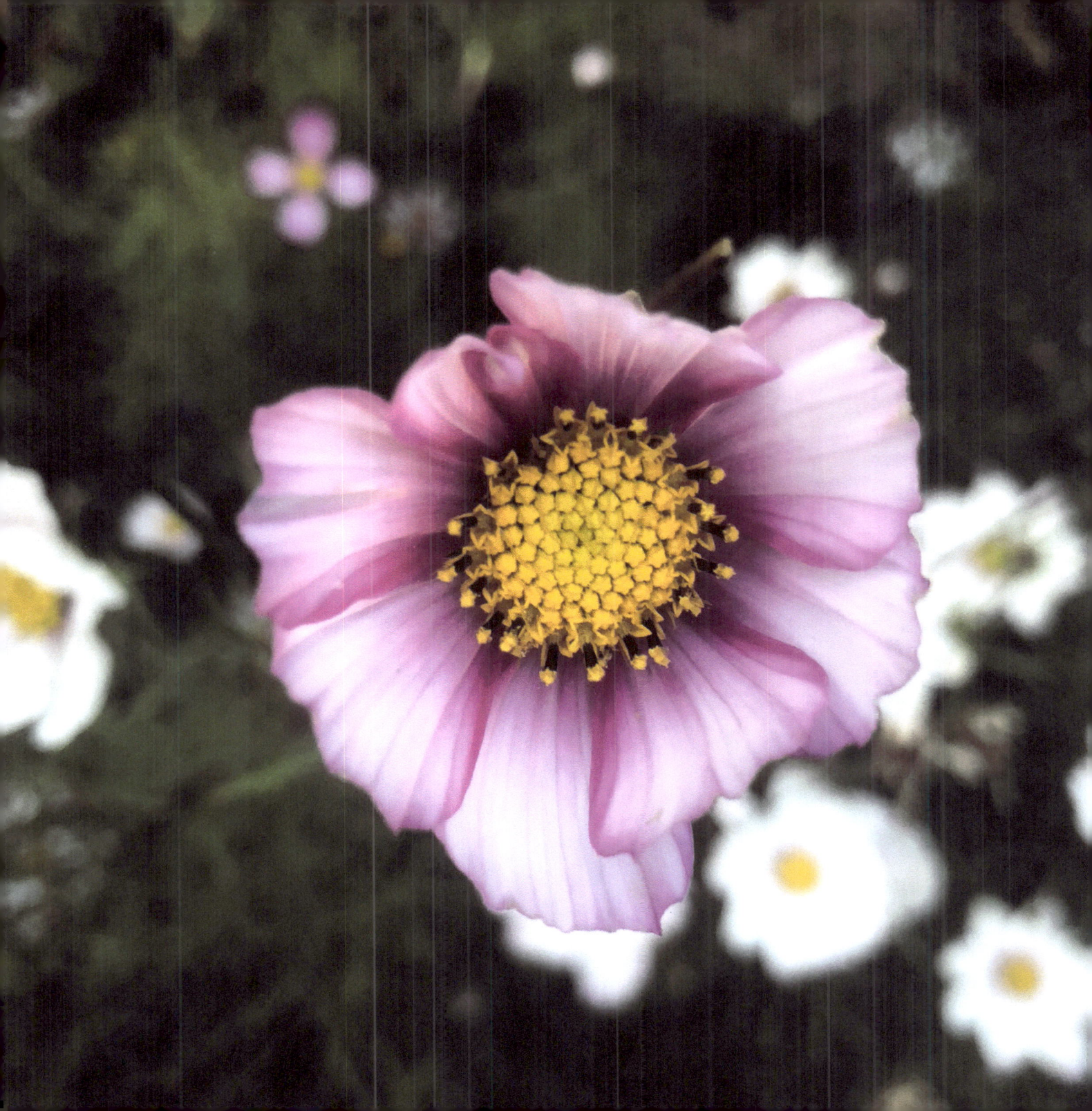

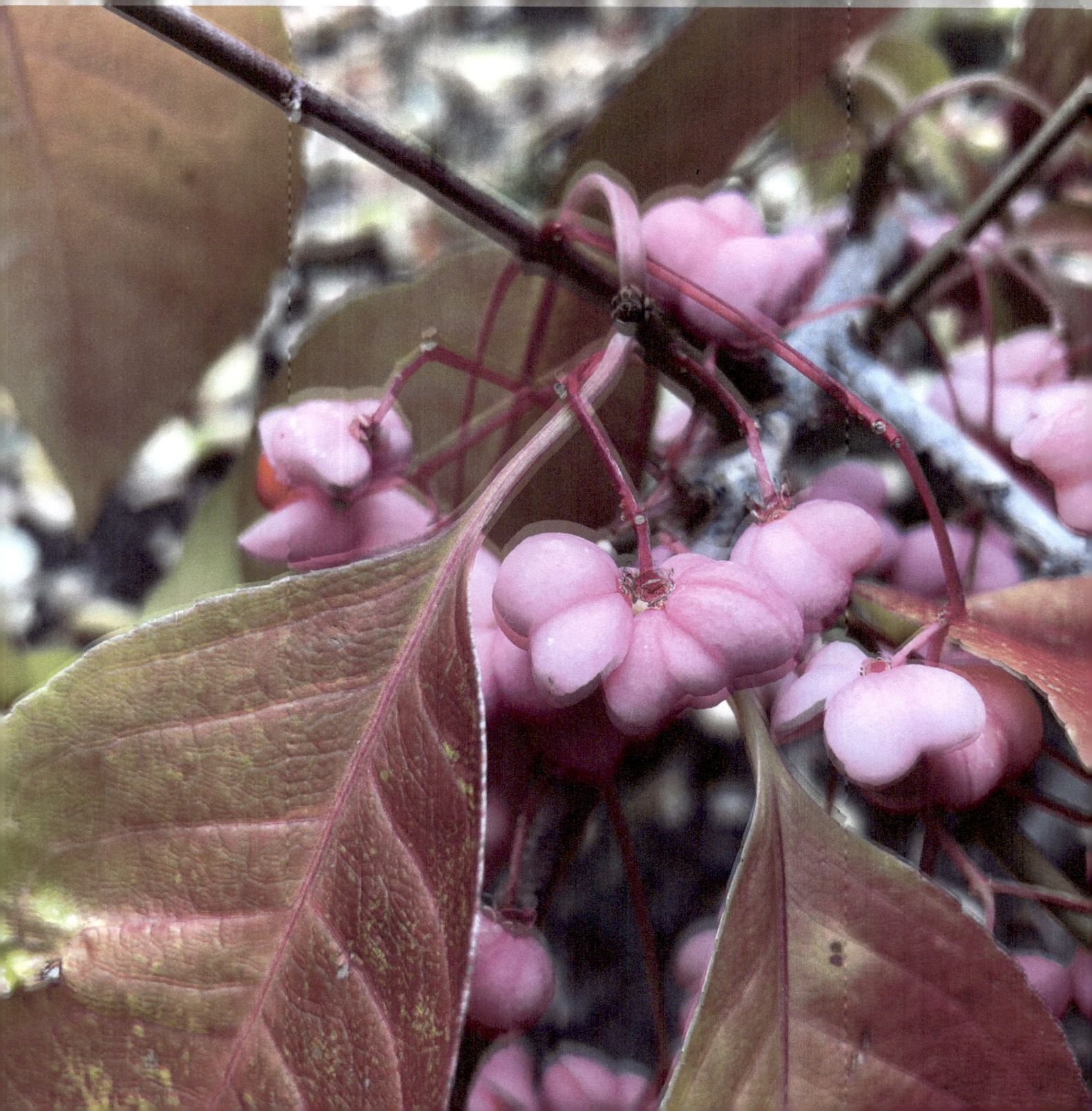

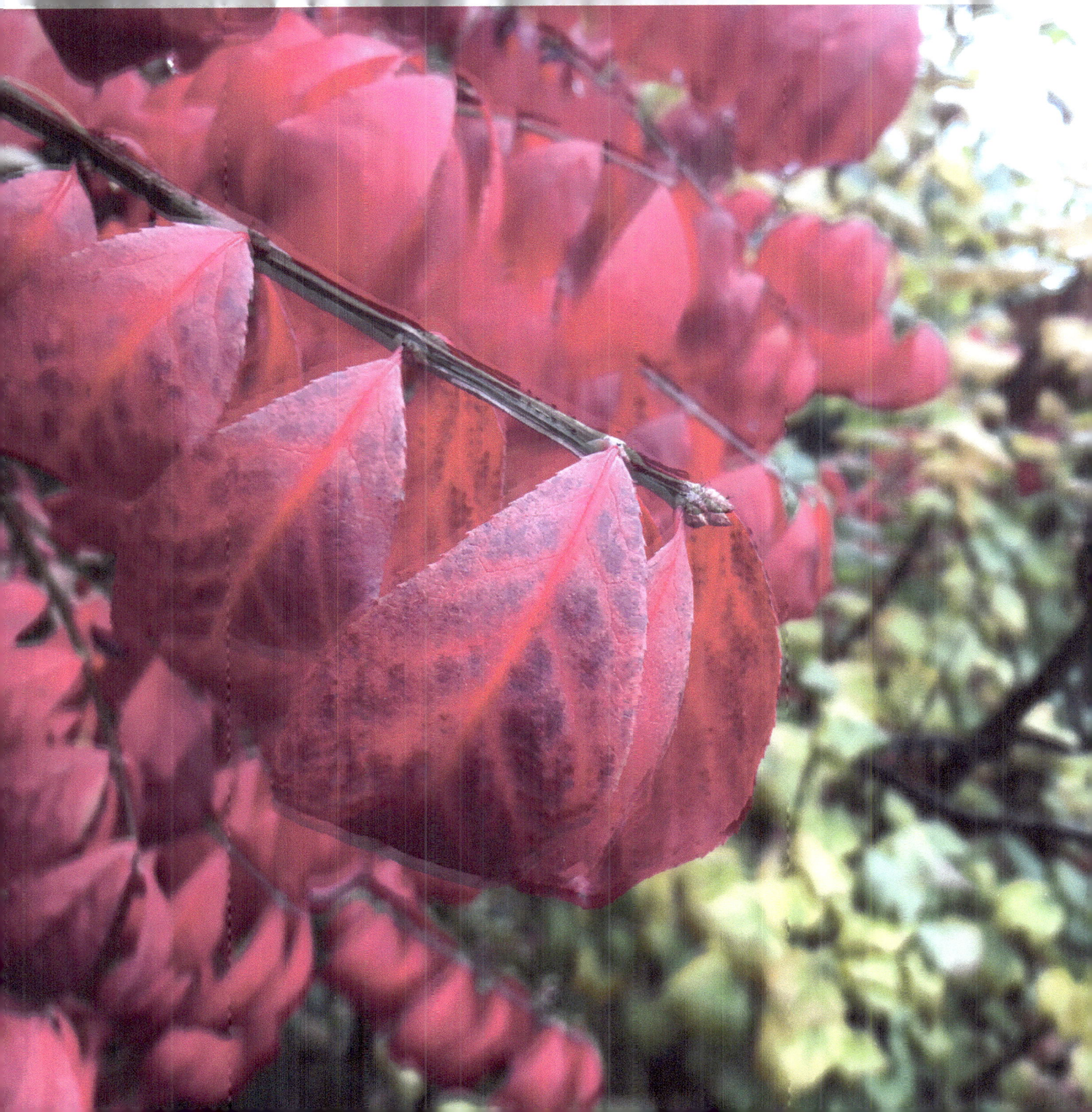

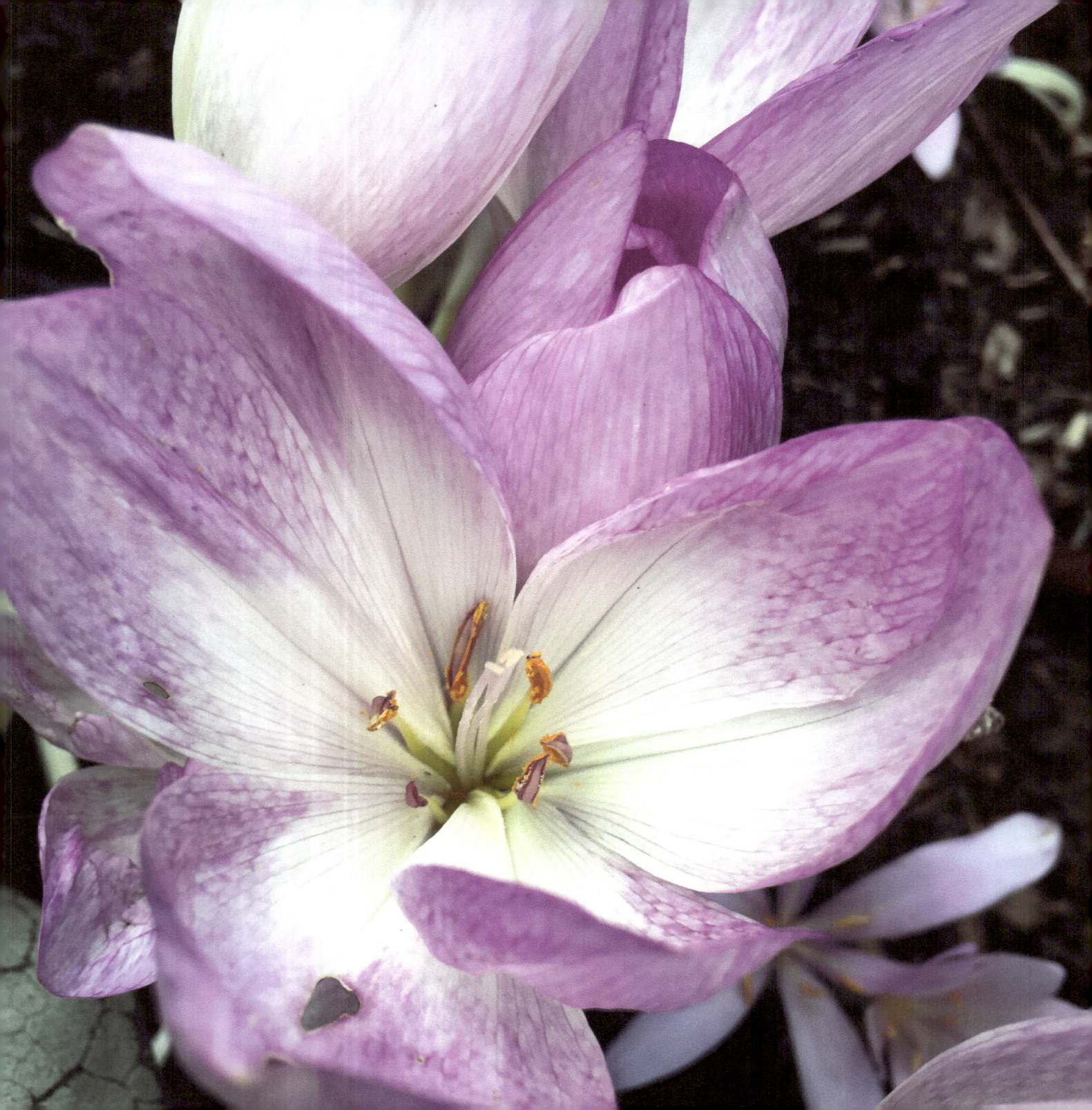

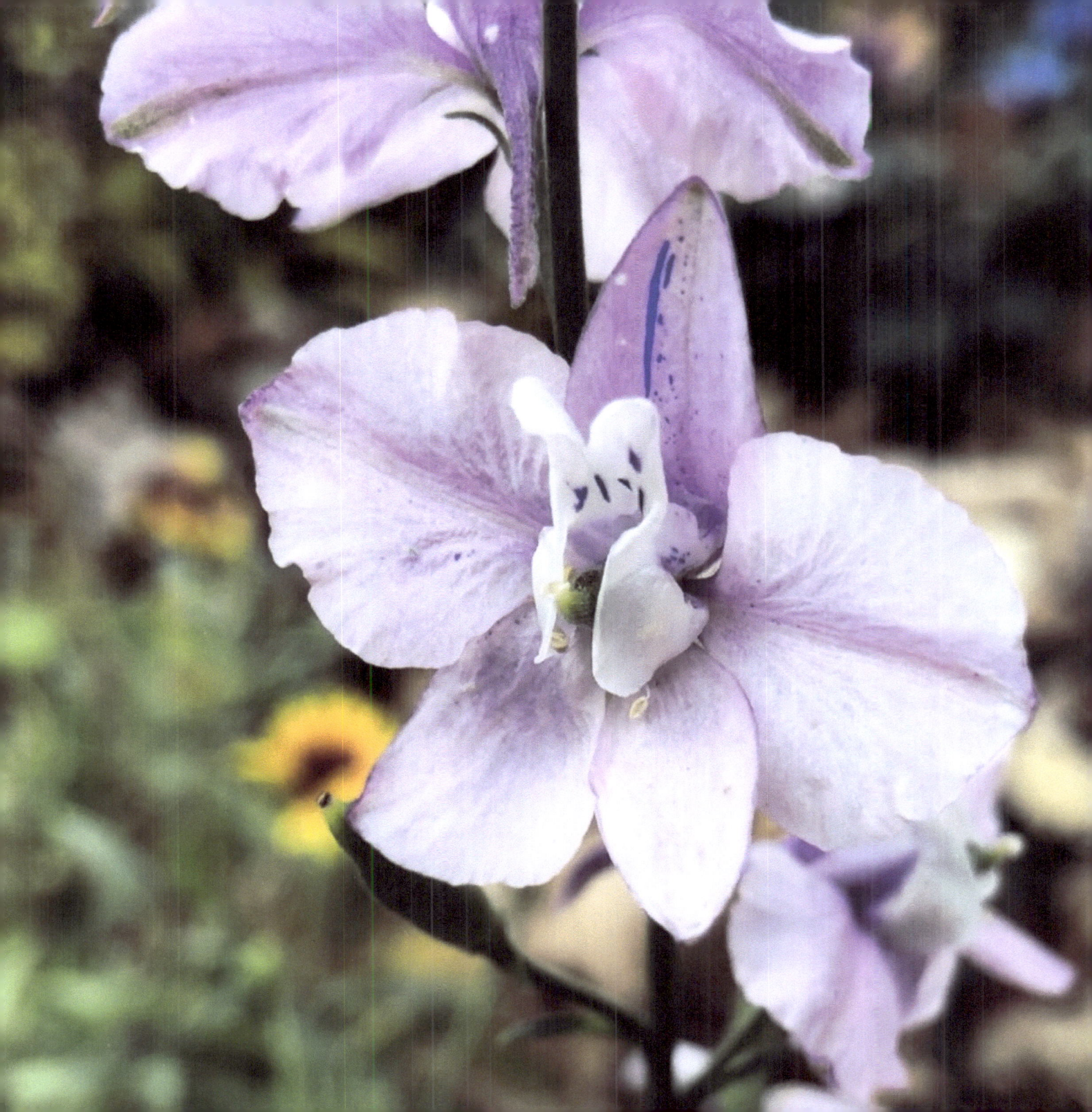

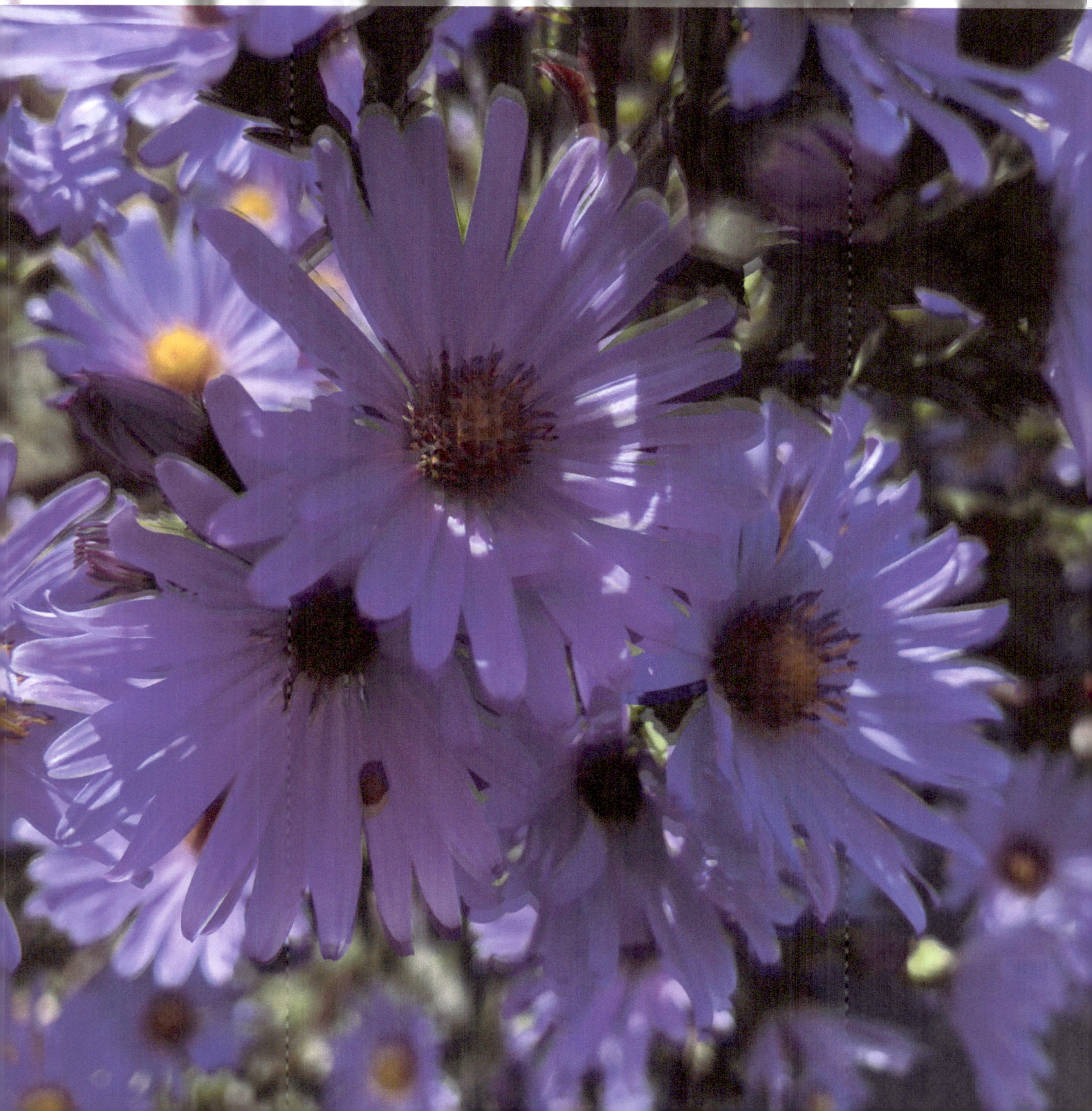

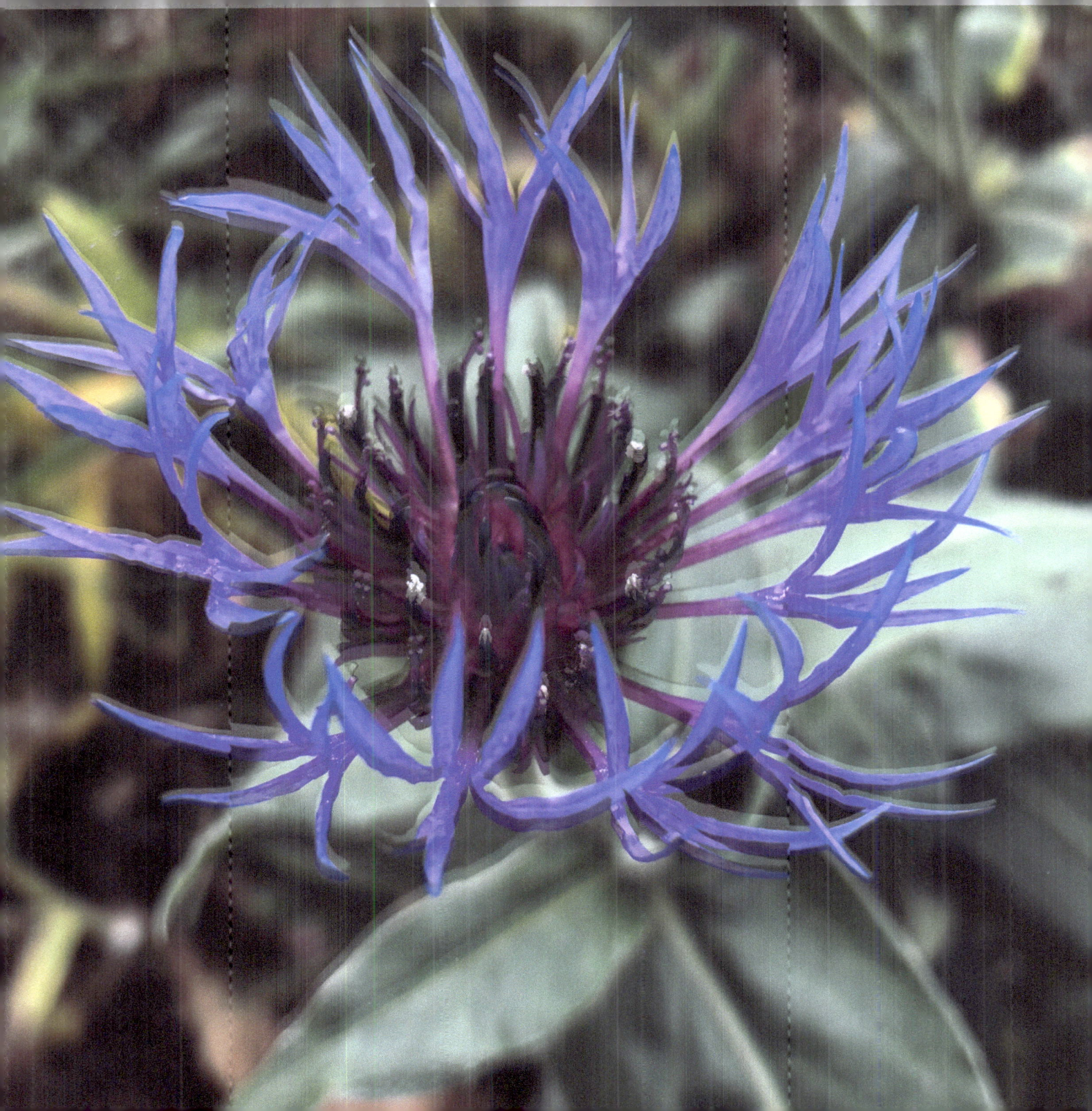

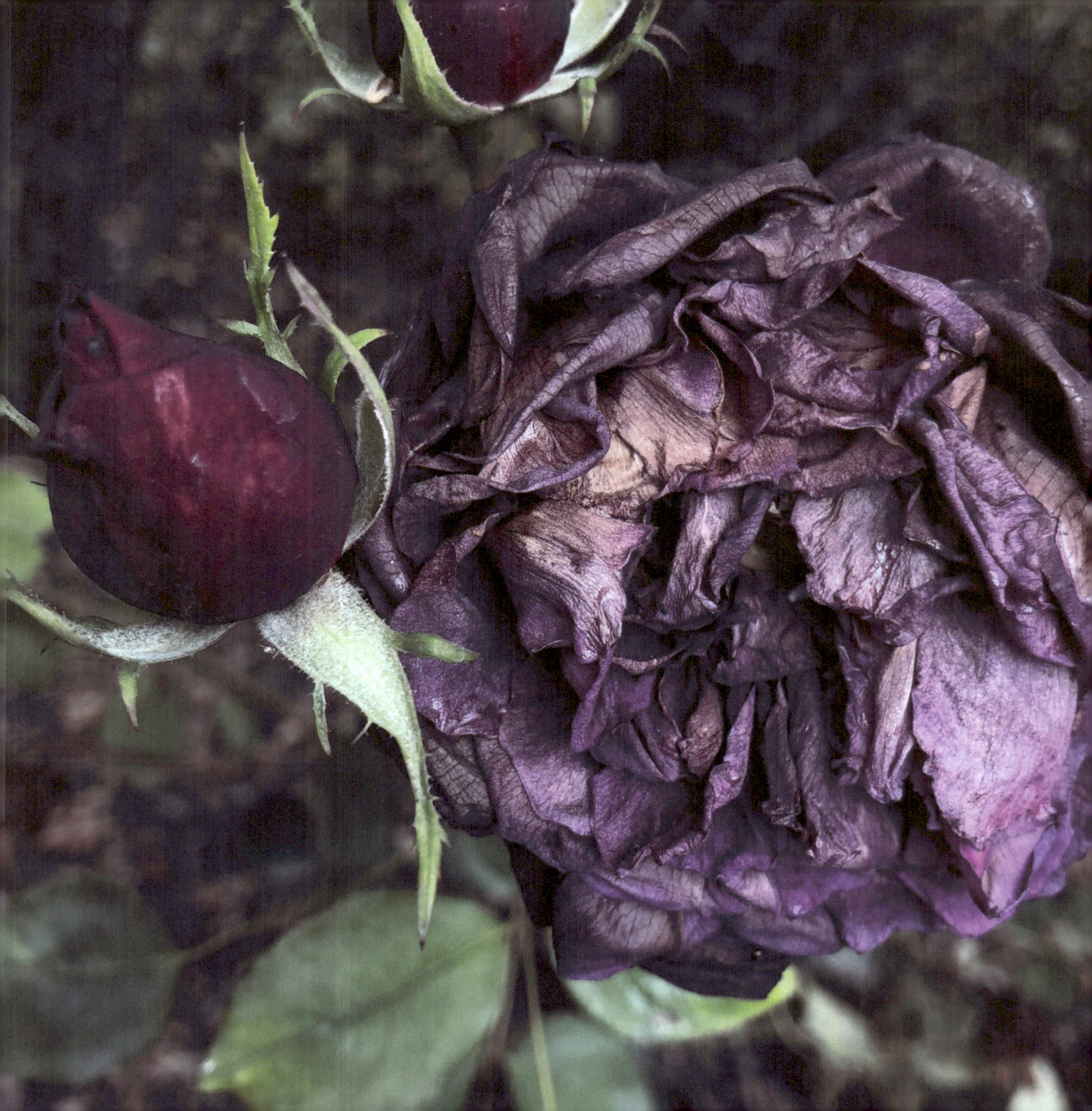

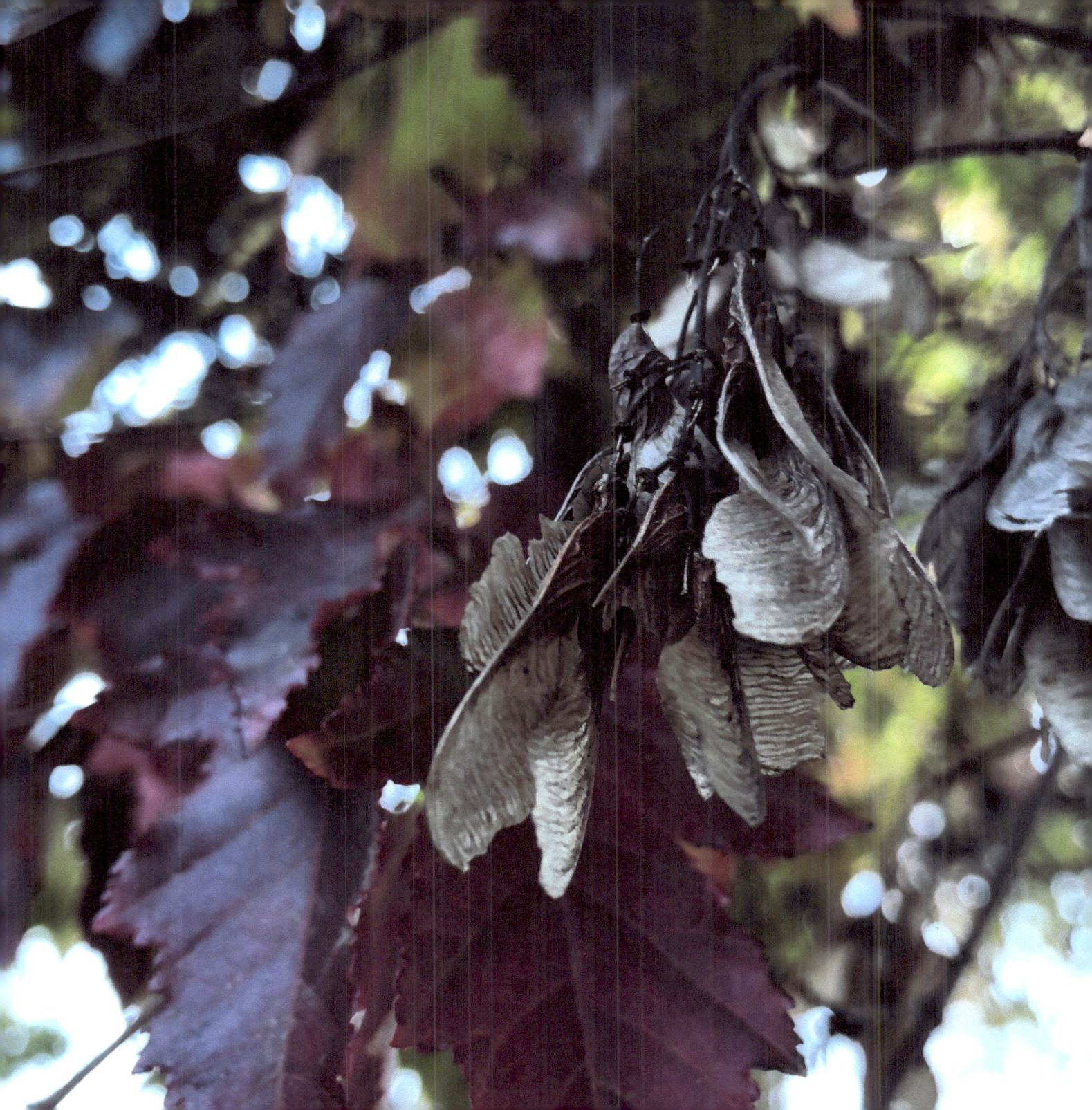

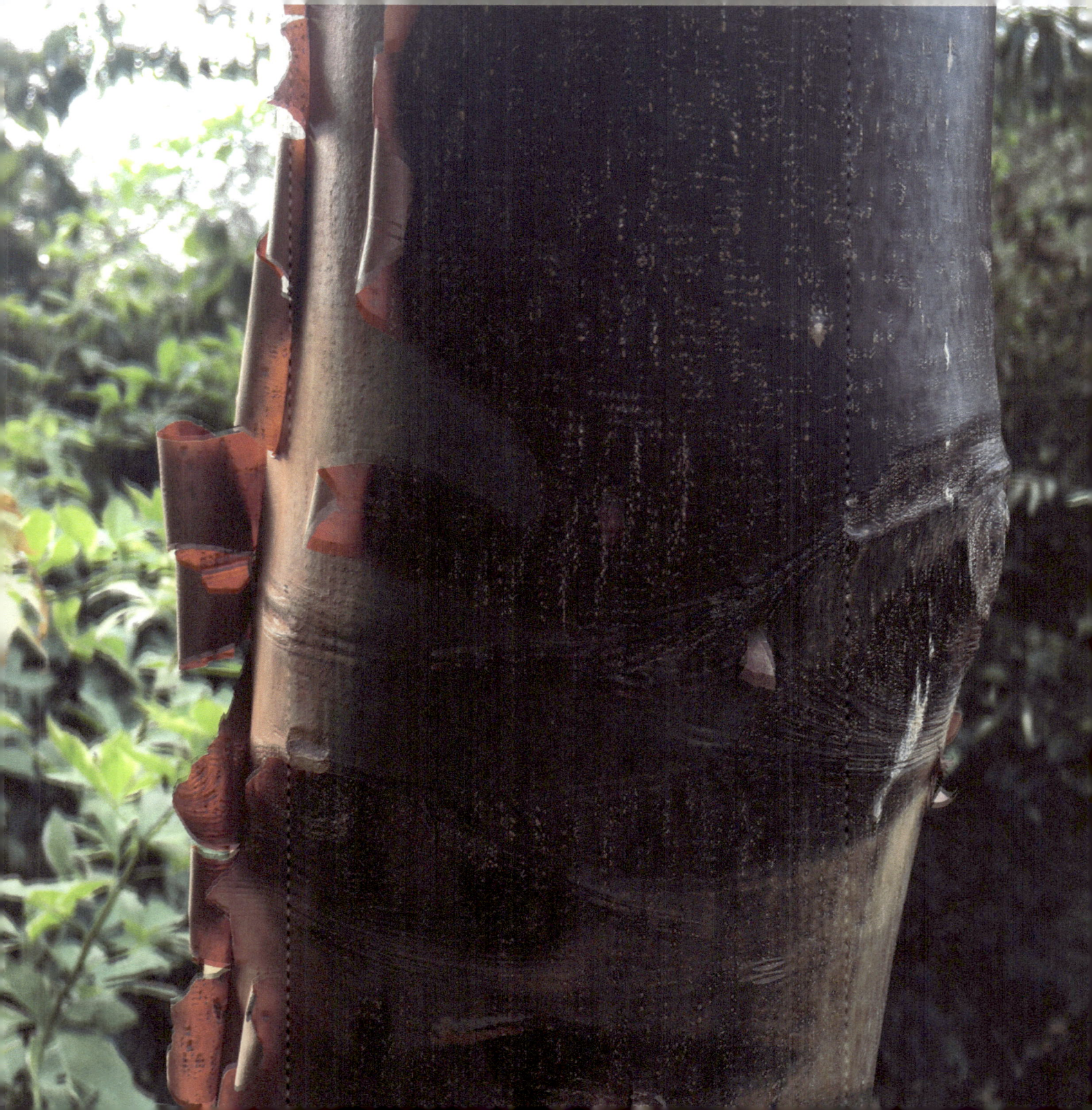

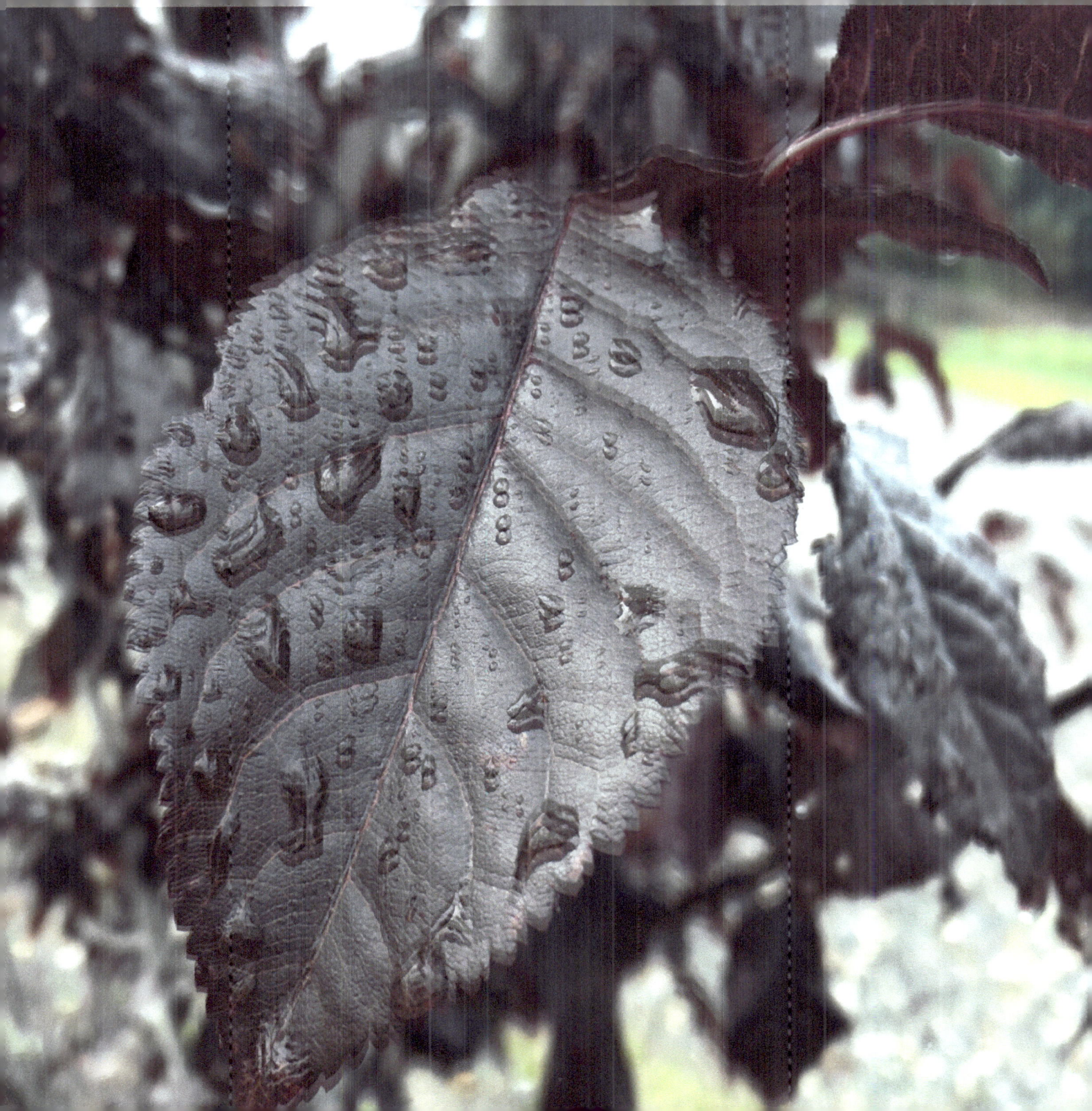

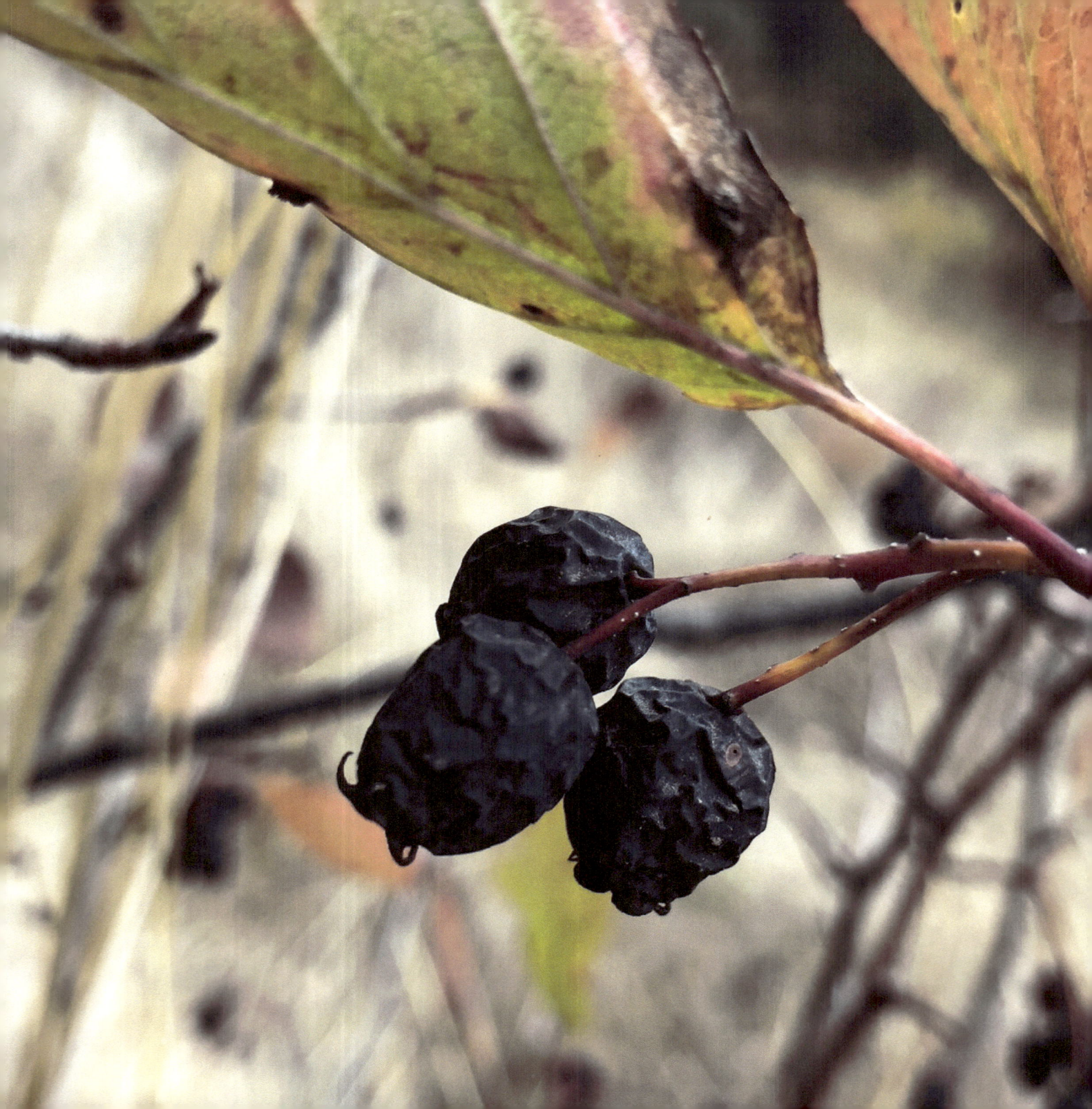

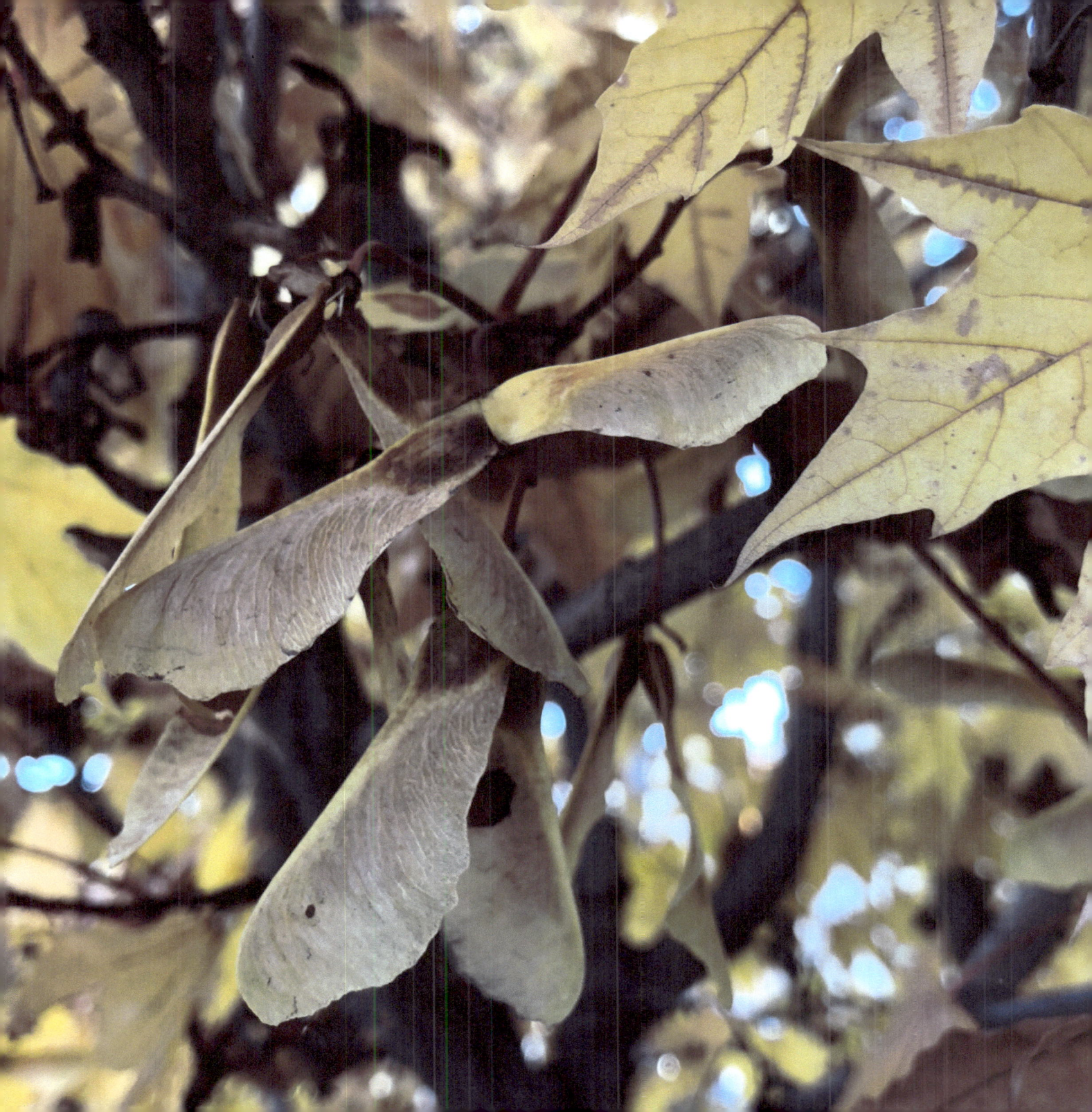

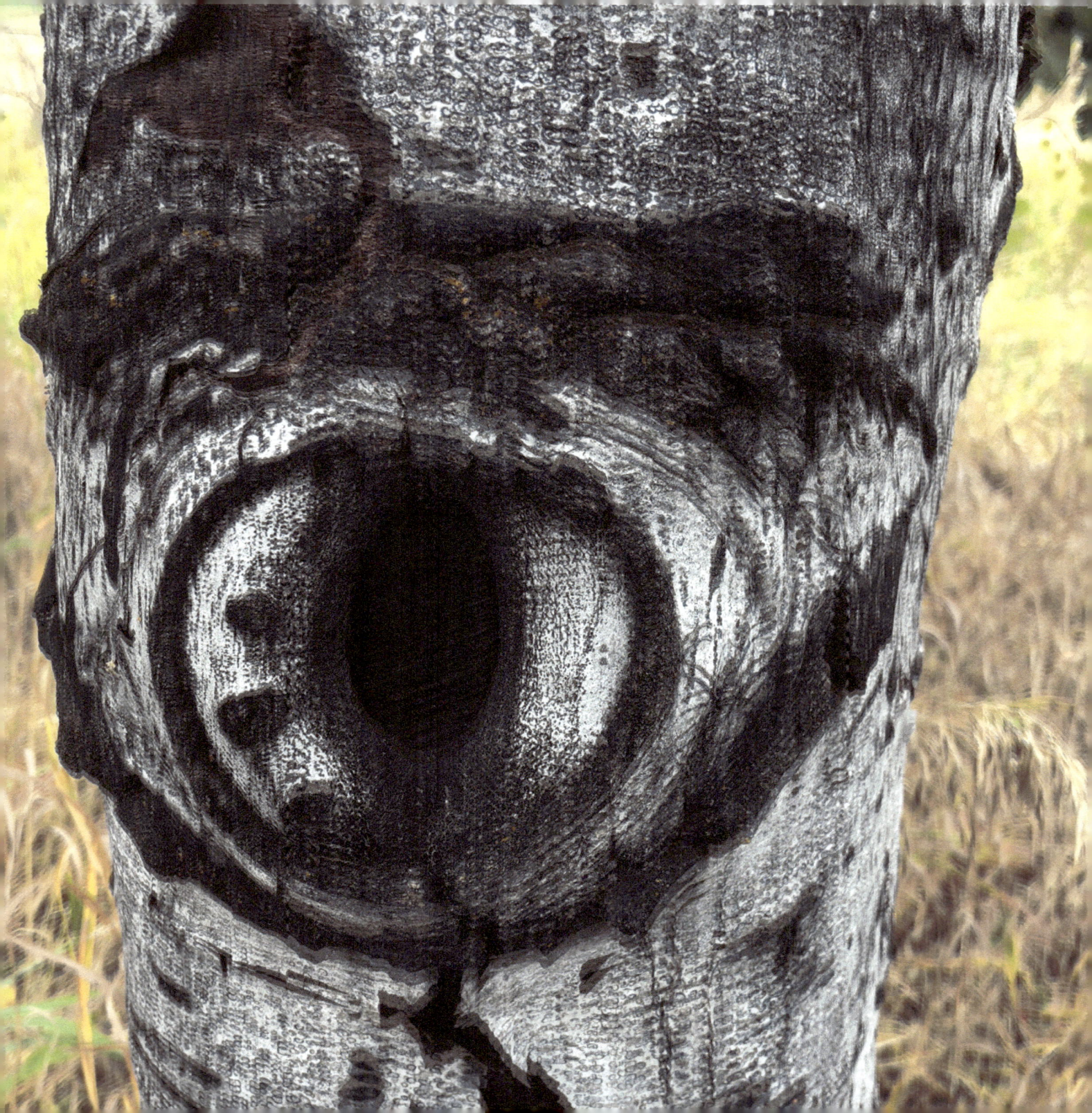

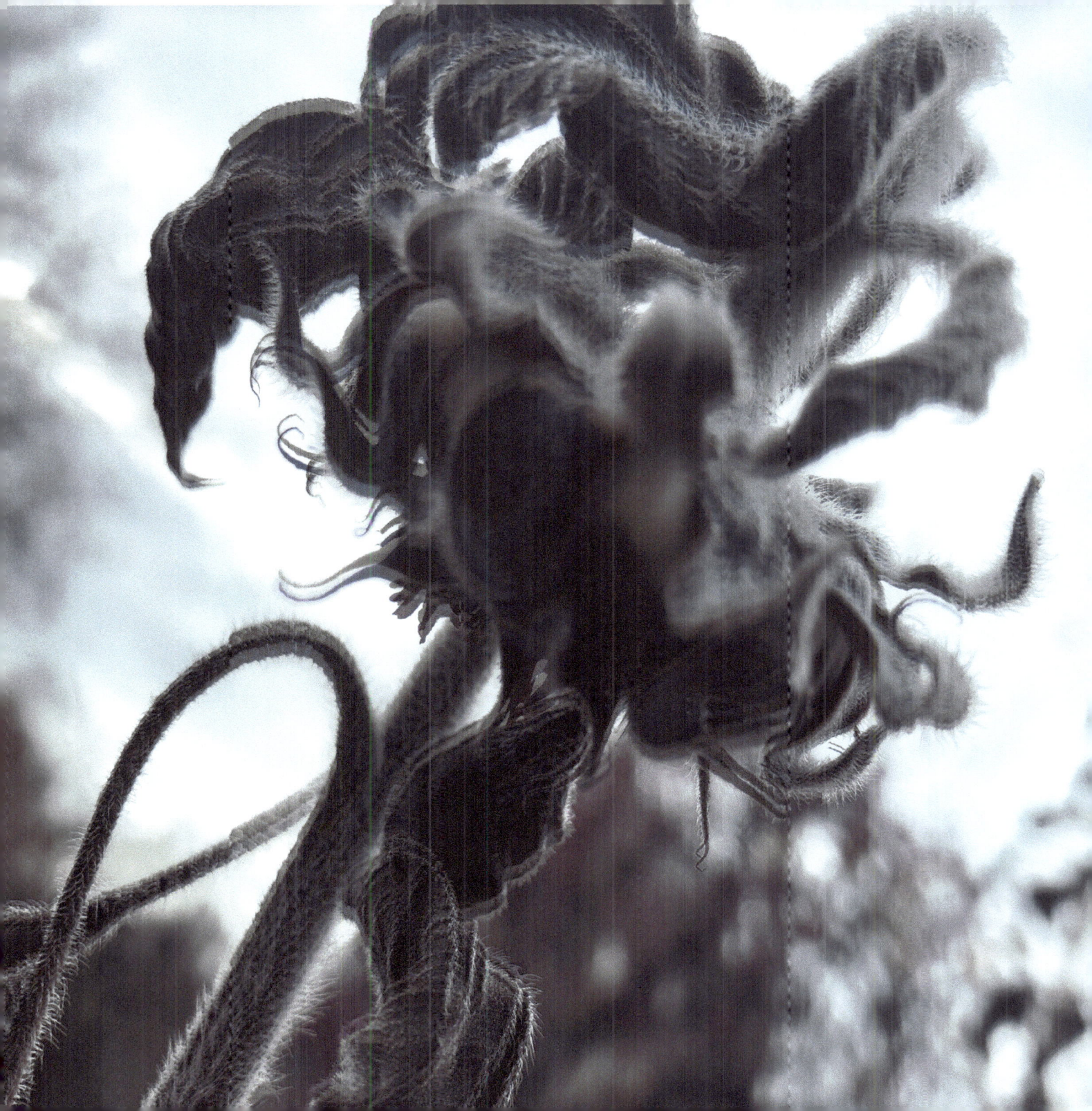

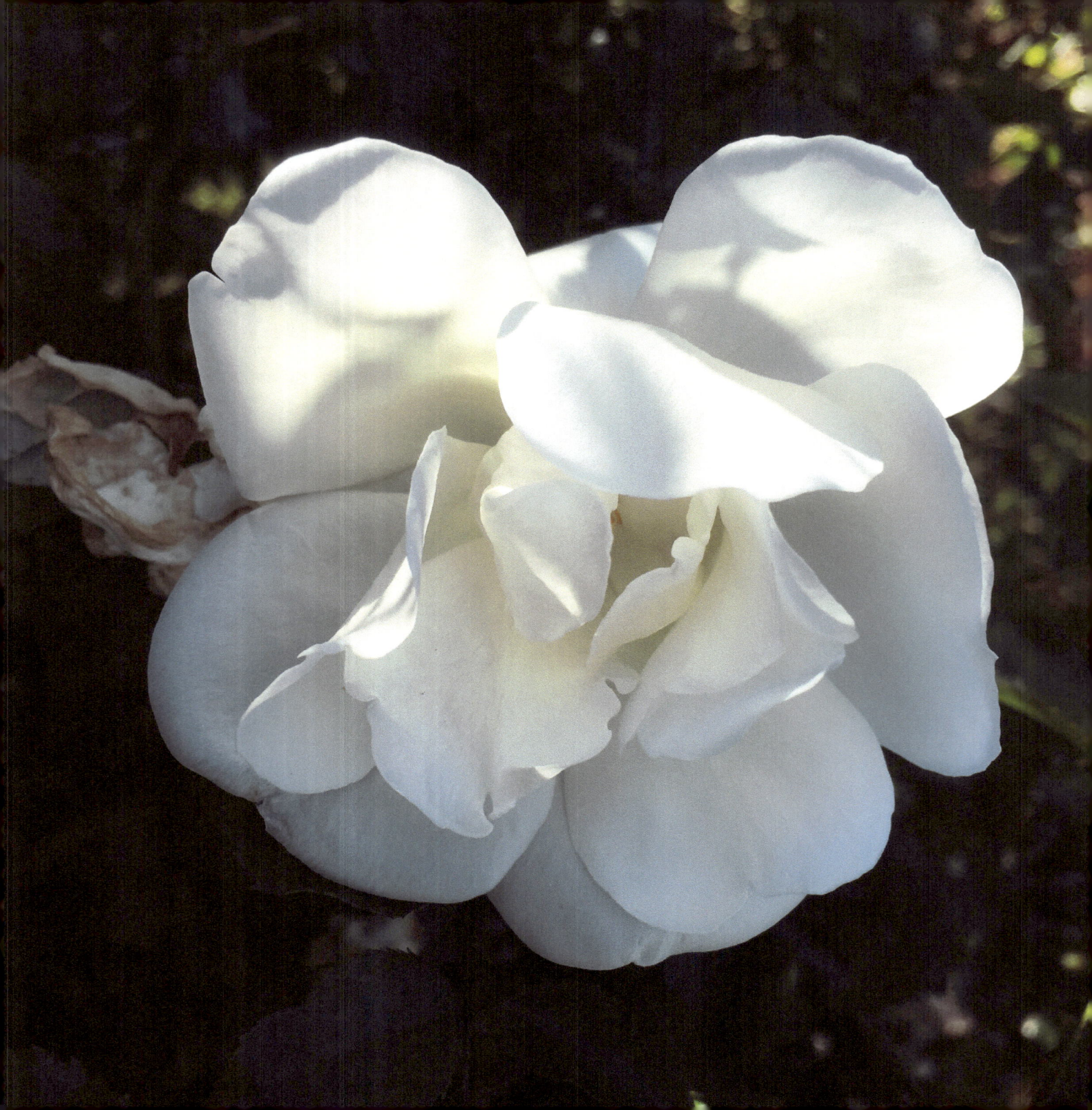

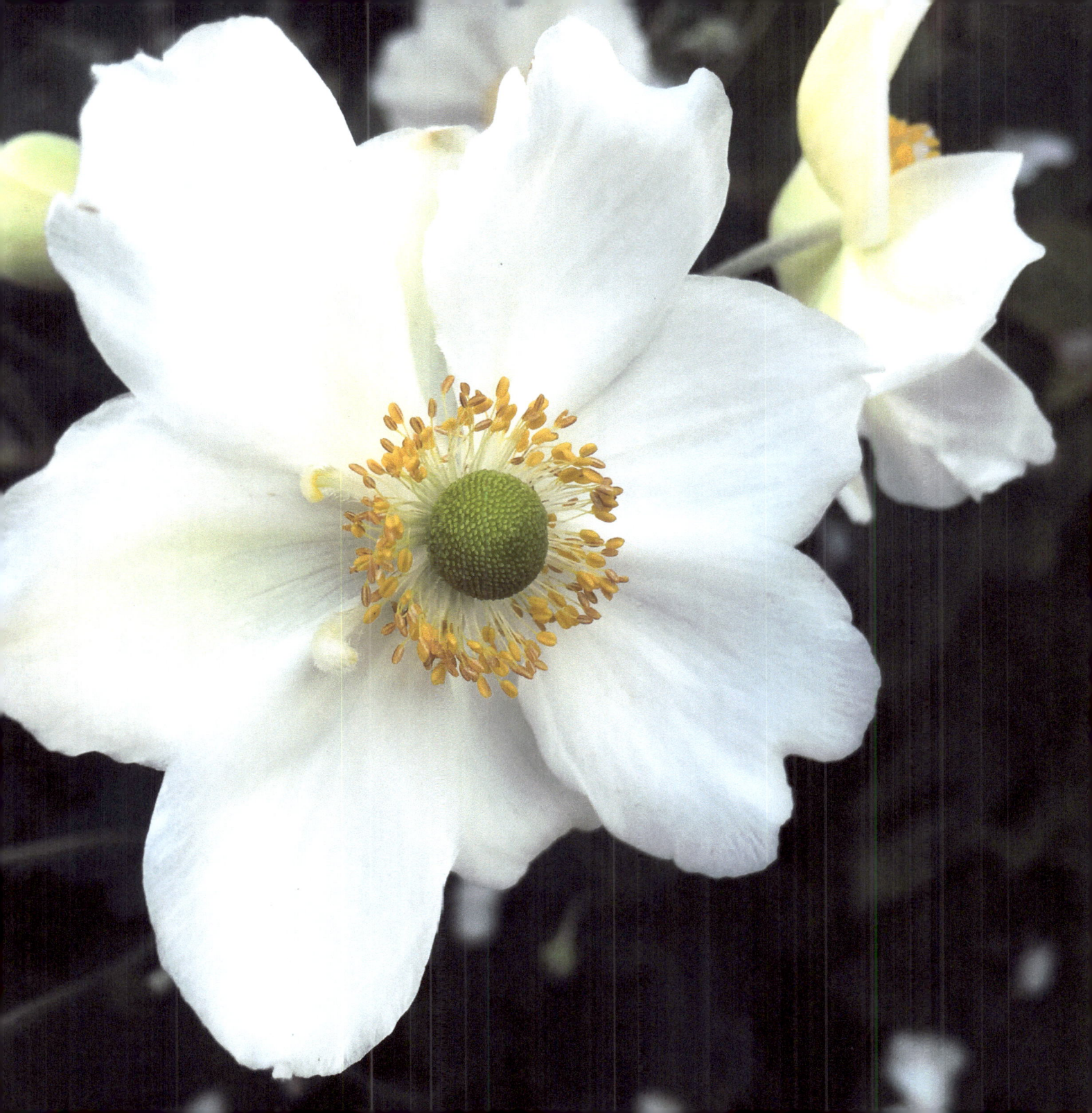

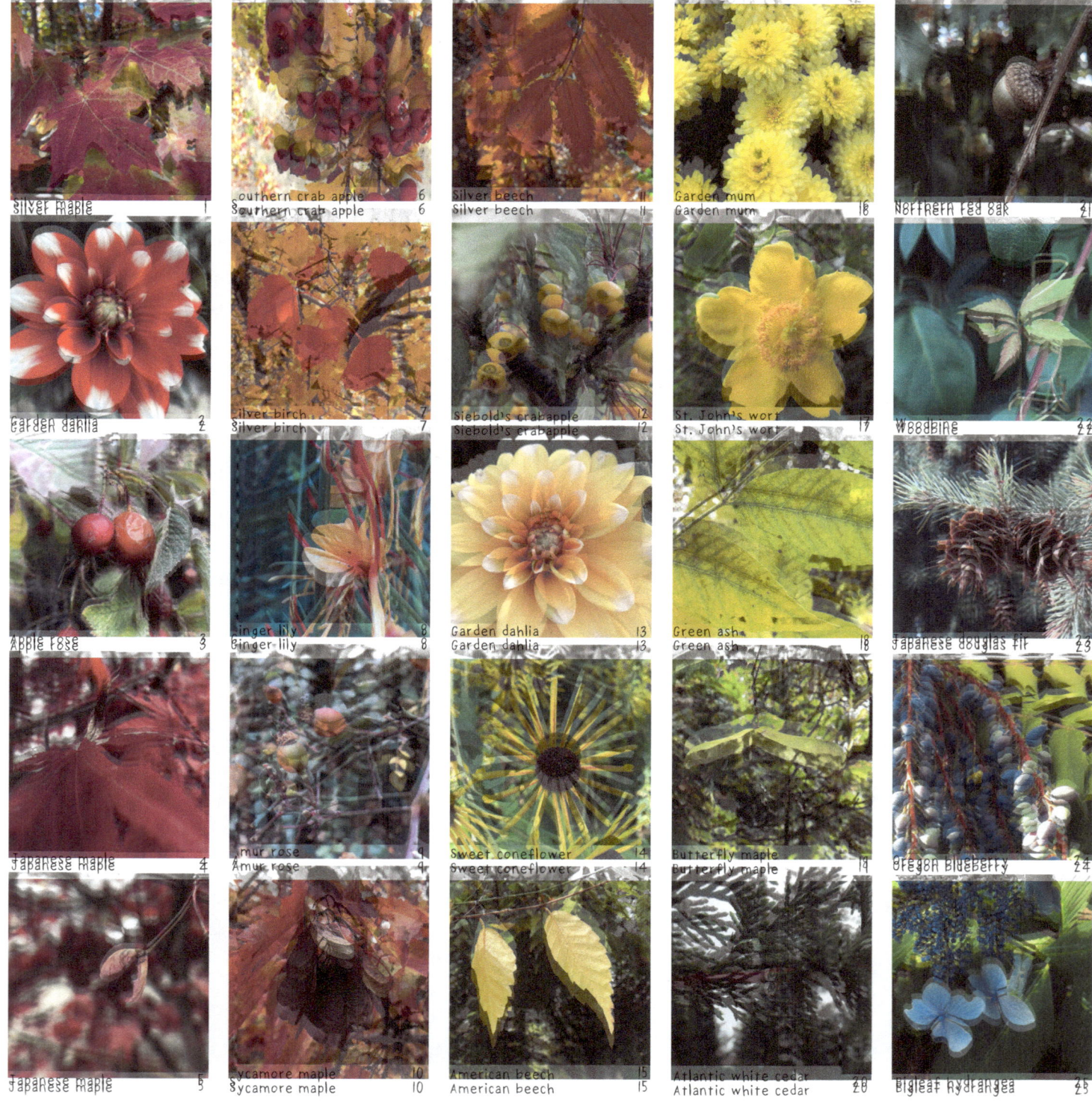

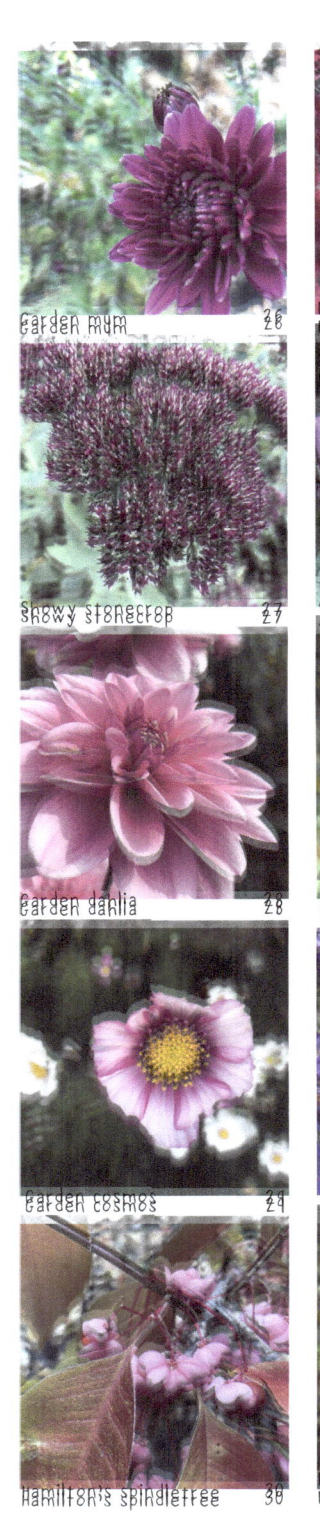
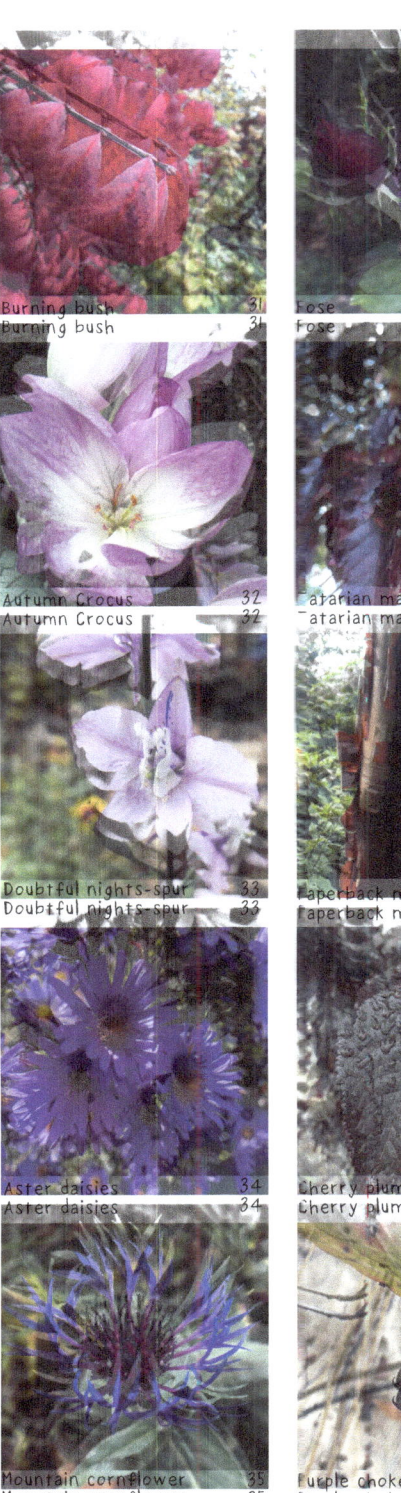
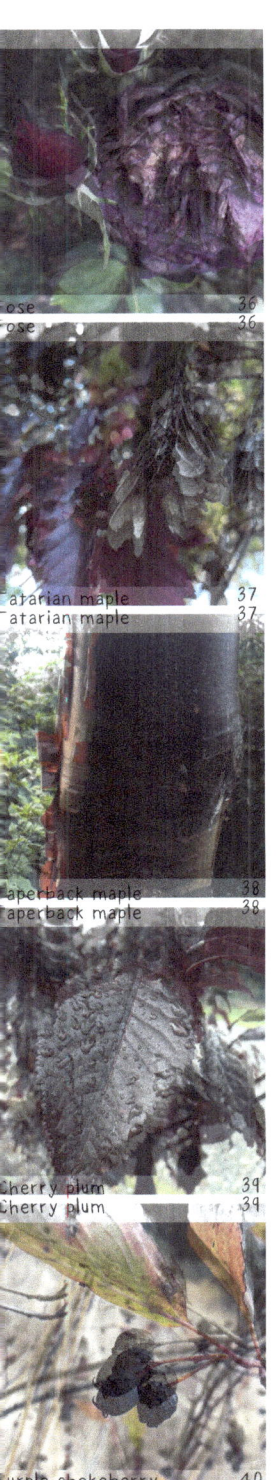
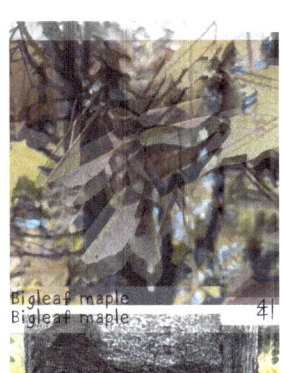

YOUR TURN
to find these **autumn** characteristics in each of the portrait photos:

leaves
1, 4, 7, 11, 15, 18, 22, 30, 31, 39

trees
38, 42

pine needles
20, 23

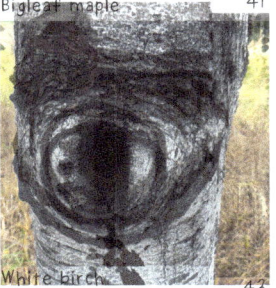

seed pods
5, 10, 19, 37, 41

pine cones
23

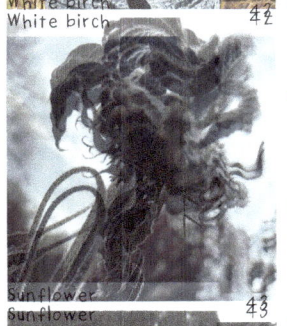

acorns
21

fruits
6, 12, 27, 40

vines
23

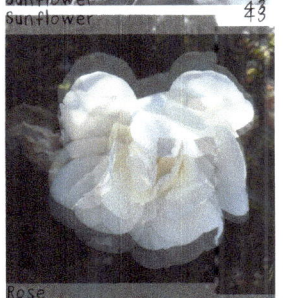

flower buds
3, 9

flowers
2, 8, 13, 14, 16, 17, 25, 26, 27, 28, 29, 30, 32, 33, 34, 35, 36, 43, 44, 45

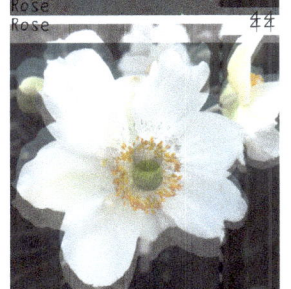

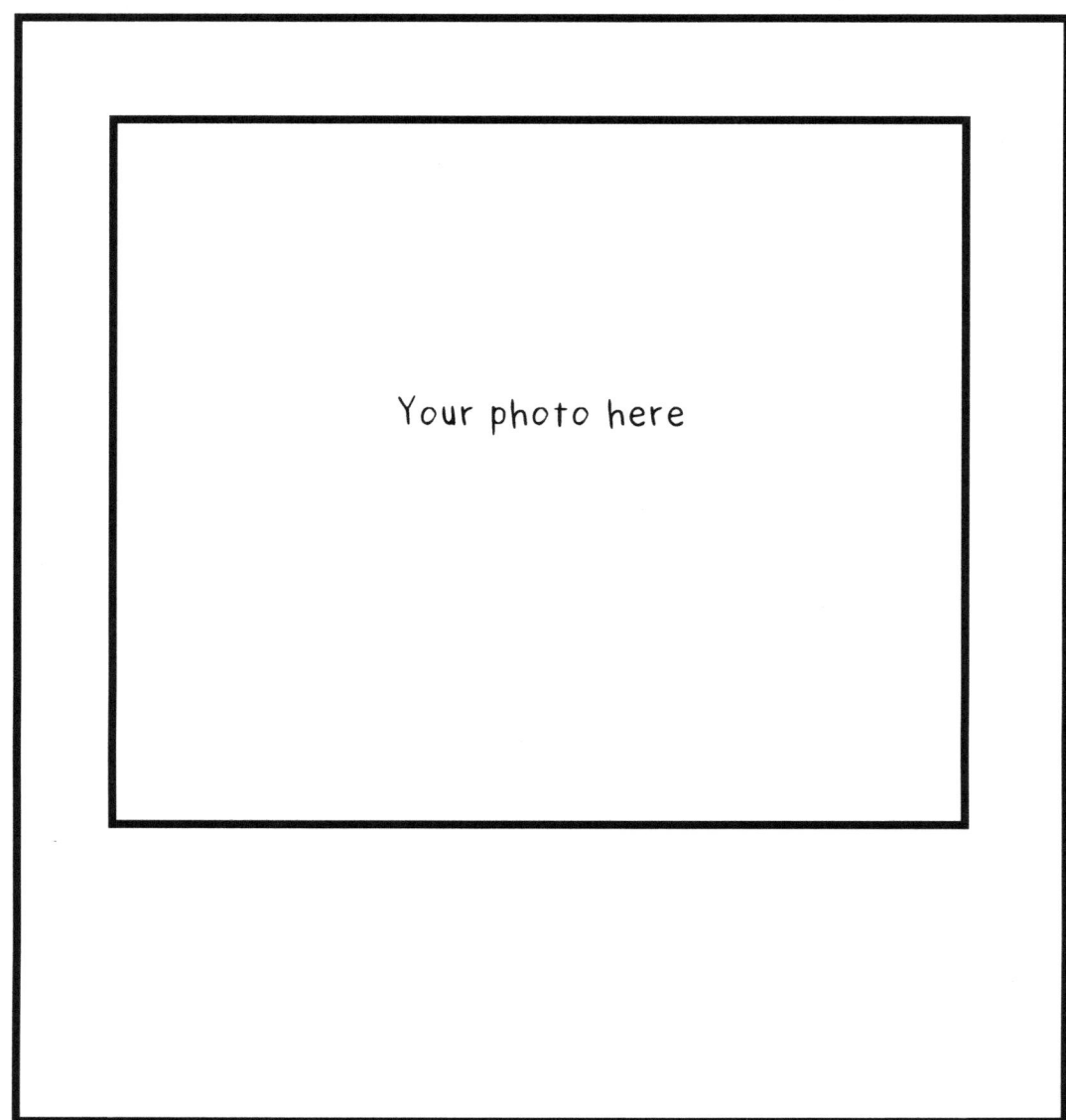

So now, YOU go & capture the **faces, characteristics** and **portraits** of nature that you see around you. I wish you well on your journey & may you start to see life in a new way.

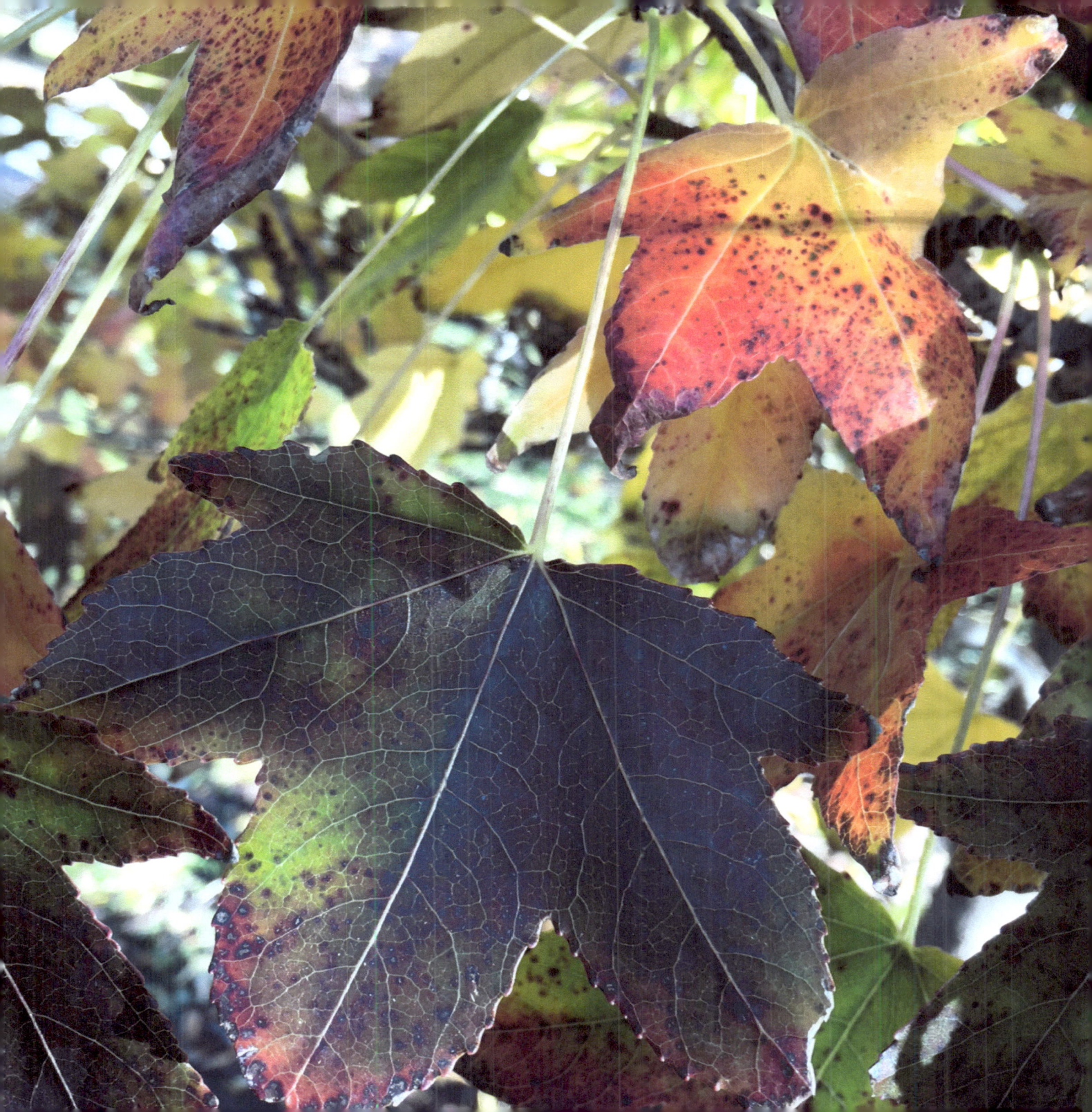